From Texting to Teaching

Don't blame technology for poor student grammar; instead, use technology intentionally to reach students and actually improve their writing! In this practical book, bestselling authors Jeremy Hyler and Troy Hicks reveal how digital tools and social media – a natural part of students' lives – can make grammar instruction more authentic, relevant, and effective in today's world.

Topics Covered:

- Teaching students to code switch and differentiate between formal and informal sentence styles
- Using flipped lessons to teach the parts of speech and help students build their own grammar guides
- Enlivening vocabulary instruction with student-produced video
- Helping students master capitalization and punctuation in different digital contexts

Each chapter contains examples, screenshots, and instructions to help you implement the ideas. With the strategies in this book, you can empower students to become better writers with the tools they already love and use daily. Additional resources and links are available on the book's companion wiki site: textingtoteaching.wikispaces.com

Jeremy Hyler is a middle school English teacher and a teacher consultant for the Chippewa River Writing Project, a satellite site of the National Writing Project. He is co-author with Troy Hicks on *Create, Compose, Connect: Reading, Writing, and Learning with Digital Tools* (Routledge, 2014).

Troy Hicks is a Professor of English and education at Central Michigan University, and Director of the Chippewa River Writing Project. He has authored or co-authored nine books, and over 30 journal articles and book chapters for teachers and other educators.

Other Eye On Education Books
Available from Routledge

From Texting to Teaching

Grammar Instruction in a Digital Age

Jeremy Hyler and Troy Hicks

Foreword by Liz Kolb

Routledge
Taylor & Francis Group

NEW YORK AND LONDON

First published 2017
by Routledge
711 Third Avenue, New York, NY 10017

and by Routledge
2 Park Square, Milton Park, Abingdon, Oxon, OX14 4RN

Routledge is an imprint of the Taylor & Francis Group, an informa business

Library of Congress Cataloging in Publication Data
Names: Hyler, Jeremy, author. | Hicks, Troy, author.
Title: From texting to teaching : grammar instruction in a digital
    age / by Jeremy Hyler and Troy Hicks.
Description: New York : Routledge, 2017. | Includes bibliographical
    references.
Identifiers: LCCN 2016053630| ISBN 9781138949270 (hardback) |
    ISBN 9781138949287 (pbk.)
Subjects: LCSH: English language—Grammar—Study and
    teaching (Middle school) | English language—Composition
    and exercises—Study and teaching (Middle school) | English
    language—Grammar—Computer-assisted instruction. | English
    language—Composition and exercises—Computer-assisted
    instruction.
Classification: LCC LB1631 .H95 2017 | DDC 428.0071/2—dc23
LC record available at https://lccn.loc.gov/2016053630

ISBN: 978-1-138-94927-0 (hbk)
ISBN: 978-1-138-94928-7 (pbk)
ISBN: 978-1-315-66916-8 (ebk)

Typeset in Palatino
by Swales & Willis Ltd, Exeter, Devon, UK

Contents

Notes on the Book

About Our Online Resources

Just as we did with *Create, Compose, Connect!*, we have created a wiki for this book. Any time in the text when we mention our "wiki," you can navigate here: textingtoteaching.wikispaces.com.

About Our Co-Authored Voice

Also, just as we did with *Create, Compose, Connect!*, we have authored this book in the first person singular, taken from Jeremy's perspective as the teacher who works with students every day. We have balanced our time, energy, and efforts on the writing, yet we hope that the book reads with a unified, coherent voice.

Dedication

To my sister Jessica, my brother-in-law Matt, and my two nieces Shelby and Taylor who continue to teach me to never give up. Thank you. – JH

To my daughter, Lexi, for whom I believe both texting and teaching will be part of your life, too. – TH

Acknowledgements

Our professional communities – at the local, state, national, and international level – support and sustain us in more ways than we can ever fully describe here. We wish to offer thanks to the many educators with whom we have discussed our work over the past few years, and we highlight just a few:

- Jeff Anderson – both of us have followed your work for years and appreciate the ways in which you are pushing all English teachers to reconsider what it means to teach editing and revision. Thanks for brainstorming some ideas with us in the early stages of this book and for your continued encouragement.
- Liz Kolb – both of us have followed your work, too, for years and we thank you for your work on the foreword, not to mention the great thinking you've shared with us through the Triple E Framework and inviting us to work with you and your team on the 4T and MACUL conferences.
- Paul Hungerford – as Jeremy's principal, we thank you for the continued professional support – both moral and financial – that allows Jeremy to do so many great things inside and outside the classroom.
- Kristen Hawley Turner – we began our conversations about this book with your concept of "digitalk" in mind, and your work to help us see kids not as deficient, but as code switchers has made a world of difference in our teaching of writing.
- Sharon Murchie and Janet Neyer, our writing group members, and Chippewa River Writing Project colleagues – thank you for your many (many!) readings of our work, as well as the thoughtful, critical, and creative suggestions along the way.
- Lauren Davis – our editor from Routledge/Eye on Education. We appreciate the ways that you offer us everything from encouraging words to careful, close editing, and everything in between.
- Lastly, we offer our thanks to one another. Every piece of writing is its own journey, and this one has had more than its fair share of twists and turns, starts and stops. Through it all, our friendship has remained strong. And, while we enjoy writing together, we have to admit that we are pleased to put this one to press . . . #bromance #happydance #endure

Meet the Authors

Jeremy Hyler is an eighth grade English and Science teacher at Fulton Middle School in Michigan. He is also co-director of the Chippewa River Writing Project at Central Michigan University and the vice-president of The Assembly for the Teaching of English Grammar (ATEG). Hyler has also co-authored *Create, Compose, Connect! Reading, Writing, and Learning with Digital Tools* (Routledge/Eye on Education, 2014) with Dr. Troy Hicks. Jeremy has also contributed chapters to other professional texts. In addition to his writings, he has presented at professional conferences in the state of Michigan as well as at the national level.

Dr. Troy Hicks is a Professor of English and Education at Central Michigan University and focuses his work on the teaching of writing, literacy and technology, and teacher education and professional development. A former middle school teacher, he collaborates with K–12 colleagues and explores how they implement newer literacies in their classrooms. Hicks directs CMU's Chippewa River Writing Project, a site of the National Writing Project, and he frequently conducts professional development workshops related to writing and technology.

Also, Hicks is author of the Heinemann titles *Crafting Digital Writing* (2013) and *The Digital Writing Workshop* (2009) as well as a co-author of *Because Digital Writing Matters* (Jossey-Bass, 2010), *Create, Compose, Connect!* (Routledge/Eye on Education, 2014), *Connected Reading* (NCTE, 2015), and *Research Writing Rewired* (Corwin Literacy, 2015). His edited collection, *Assessing Students' Digital Writing* (Teachers College Press, 2015) features the work of seven National Writing Project teachers. Hicks has authored or co-authored over 30 journal articles and book chapters.

In March 2011, Hicks was honored with CMU's Provost's Award for junior faculty who demonstrate outstanding achievement in research and creative activity and, in 2014, he was honored with the Conference on English Education's Richard A. Meade Award for scholarship in English Education.

Foreword

Liz Kolb, Ph.D.

UNIVERSITY OF MICHIGAN

"We have done our students a disservice when it comes to teaching grammar. Let's catch up to the current debate by pushing forward . . . and watch as history takes another turn." – Jeremy Hyler and Troy Hicks

Take everything you thought you knew about grammar and toss it out the window! This book will inspire you to re-think how you approach both teaching and learning with grammar. When I was asked to write this foreword, I honestly thought, "how can a book about grammar be remotely interesting"? Jeremy Hyler and Dr. Troy Hicks prove grammar has a fascinating history, and there are intriguing debates on grammar use that still persist today.

At the beginning of the book, Hyler and Hicks brilliantly weave together a captivating historical perspective on grammar. They are able to connect the traditional instructional practices around grammar, while juxtaposing how modern day technological advances have impacted the way we both perceive and engage with grammar in the digital age. What struck me was the authors' honesty; they fully acknowledge their own frustration with "text speak" or "digitalk" in student writing. Yet, when they dug deeper into the impact of informal talk on formal writing, they found that the empirical research has shown that little of it has trickled over into formal writing. Furthermore, there are benefits for students as they learn to "code switch" between cultural norms of texting and formal academic grammar. This is just one example of the many preconceived ideas that society has about students, grammar and the digital age which the authors astutely address and debunk.

Like many reading this book, I grew up learning grammar as an isolated discipline. Memorizing the difference between a noun and a verb, or understanding when to use a semicolon versus a colon. As a student, I found this "drill and practice" approach to grammar dull and uninspiring. I often feared grammar, worrying about having a comma out of place and having a smart-mouthed peer or teacher correct me in a know-it-all manner. Refreshingly, Hyler and Hicks do not view grammar as a linear or isolated discipline, rather the book is a journey into how grammar can be woven into authentic experiences. In particular, the authors take full advantage of the digital age to "add value" to the process of allowing grammar learning to become a natural extension of student life, rather than using technology to "drill and kill" grammar learning with gimmicky games or unrelated rewards. They argue that "It is still our responsibility as educators to deliver grammar instruction effectively and not just use technology for the sake of using it; instead, we can help students use technology in meaningful and effective ways that can empower them to become better writers" (p. 25). The authors justify why we should apply technology to support grammar learning with the ISTE standards, Common Core ELA standards, and the significance of the revision and editing process in literacy learning. Hyler and Hicks not only give an argument of a more authentic way to learn grammar that makes sense in our digitally-connected world, but they provide educators with practical and useful tools to employ a collaborative approach to grammar with technology tools.

In order to measure the benefit that technology tools may bring to grammar learning, the authors smartly make use of the Triple E Framework. I developed the Triple E Framework in 2011 at the University of Michigan for the exact purpose that the authors are employing: to assess how well technology tools add value to learning goals, rather than measuring the "fun" or sophistication of the technology tool. The framework is based on education technology research over the past two decades. Evidence-based research on technology tools has shown that positive learning gains can occur when technology is integrated using effective instructional strategies. These strategies include co-engagement, authentically connecting student learning and everyday life experiences, engaging students in higher-cognitive thinking (for example: hypothesis, inquiry, creation) rather than drill and practice, and having students actively involved in the learning process to meet learning goals (time-on-task). The Triple E Framework reflects this research and measures when these evidence-based practices are happening through and with technology tools. Jeremy Hyler and Troy Hicks understand the nuanced difference between using technology to "engage" because it is shiny and fun, and using technology to enhance and extend to learning. This book is full of practical ideas of the latter.

As you read the book, you will notice the words "authentic," "collaborative," and "process" threaded throughout the chapters. You would be hard-pressed to find a historical period when grammar and these words have been used together. Effective technology use stems from elevating the learning to co-engagement, real-world connections, and a focus on the learning process (not the product). For example, having a student publish a podcast is lovely and fun, but it is actually in the process of scripting, editing, and revising the podcast that the majority of learning actually occurs – not in the finished piece. While many educators skip right to the beautiful publication and forget to emphasize the process of learning, this book does it right, understanding that the process of learning comes before the finished product.

The authors are asking educators to recognize the fact that students are living in a digital world. Instead of ignoring or being frustrated by the "code switching" that students engage in with grammar, the authors ask teachers to embrace it. Students should learn how to integrate this multimodal and mobile world of digital text into their academic learning and understanding of grammar. Furthermore, debate and discussion on grammar use should be encouraged, rather than a focus on mechanical memorization and traditional assessment on the use of grammar.

Thankfully, the approach to grammar learning that Hyler and Hicks promote in this book is not the way I learned in my 2nd grade classroom in 1982. I am not familiar with many of the strategies that the authors are encouraging; rather my memory is full of dull drill and practice quizzes and scary red ink pens. Yet, after reading the book, for the first time in my life, I find myself enjoying and understanding the authentic use of grammar as it relates to my digital life. I am betting that you, and more importantly, your students, will too!

1

What's the Matter with the Teaching of Grammar?

For what seems like forever, teachers have struggled to teach grammar and students have struggled to learn it. I recently confirmed this in my own classroom with a quick survey. Here are some (very) brief highlights of my students' thoughts about grammar instruction:

- ◆ Boring
- ◆ Stupid
- ◆ Pointless
- ◆ Definitely not fun

Sound familiar? Yes, these are all students' opinions of grammar instruction, and I am sure that your students feel much the same.

Let's face it, we are working with students today who do not find grammar instruction engaging, and perhaps some of us have been working with these same students for years or decades! Moreover, let's face another truism: many of us don't find the teaching of grammar all that interesting either. In some ways, this should come as no surprise. Over the past century, there have been numerous studies exploring how grammar gets taught in English classrooms and how students learn what grammar concepts are presented to them, if they learn anything at all. While a full accounting of these reports could be a book in and of itself, Troy and I (Jeremy) have gathered quite a few, and I will offer a few highlights from the history of teaching grammar below.

I do so because, as an English teacher, it is critical to know where our profession has been in order to make informed, intelligent, decisions about where to go next. Of course, a major part of where we want to go next, as it relates to teaching grammar involves technology, a topic we will take up in Chapter 2 where I will describe my journey toward using technology more thoroughly. And, let's make one thing clear – I am not using technology just as a hook to make grammar more engaging. As with any use of technology in teaching, I am thinking about different ways to help my students make connections to other ideas they have learned and explore their own literacy practices. Using Liz Kolb's Triple E Framework for technology integration, I will make my purposes for using all kinds of tools like social media, video, and mobile apps, quite clear throughout the entire book.

Just like we did in *Create, Compose, Connect!*, Troy and I will explore a number of technologies and approaches to teaching using the singular voice. I've tried these strategies in my classroom, and then he and I have had extensive discussions about what's worked, as well as what hasn't. This book is a collaborative effort, and we both appreciate the ways it has helped grow our friendship and professional ties.

Also, similar to our first book, the process of writing has – in and of itself – helped us both revise and refine our thinking. When we made the initial pitch on this book, we knew it would have something to do with grammar and technology. Over time and by thinking about the work of two leaders in our field – Jeff Anderson and his approach to revising, as well as Liz Kolb and her approach to integrating technology – Troy and I were able to shape the focus of this book.

Thus, *From Texting to Teaching* was born. We considered the many ways in which our colleagues see the devices in our students' hands (for texting, or other forms of social media) and how we need to refocus on what we can do with these tools for teaching. Also, we don't want to move students away from their own literacy practices with these tools. Texting, posting, commenting, sharing, and many other processes make up what it is that our tweens and teens now do with their mobile devices. Yet, there are many more activities that we can invite – and encourage – our students to do with a different approach to teaching.

Just as I used to be part of the "cell phone brigade" and wanted to take students' phones away and had to shift my thinking on that stance, I have also needed to change my approach to teaching students about the ways in which they employ the English language when using their devices. Along with Jeff Anderson and Liz Kolb, you will see many other writers that have pushed my thinking, including Kristen Hawley Turner and her work on "digitalk." I've realized that our language is always evolving, that I do not need to be some kind of grammar police, and that we can, indeed, teach grammar in thoughtful, productive ways when using technology. Because, as our students note, "boring," "stupid," "pointless," and "definitely not fun" doesn't seem like a good way to go.

More importantly, Troy and I have been looking at what our professional organizations – including the National Council of Teachers of English, and one of its constituent groups, the Assembly for English Grammar – as well as many of our colleagues have been saying for many years: rote grammar instruction doesn't work. So, before we do anything to talk about technology and grammar instruction, I want to outline what I've learned about the teaching of grammar and how it has informed the stance I take today. In doing so, you can get a sense of the many conversations that Troy and I have had in the past two years as we've developed this book, and the many lesson ideas within it.

In other words: what's the matter with grammar? Let's find out a bit about our history, so we can begin to shape the future of teaching grammar together.

The Great Grammar Debate, Part 1: 1890s to 1990s

Should we explicitly teach grammar in English class?

Or, should we work with students to learn grammar in context?

Or, are there other paths?

These are questions that have been part of our profession for decades. Regardless of what we call it, grammar (including "usage," or the "rules" that govern the proper use of language as well as "mechanics," the actual nuts and bolts of spelling, capitalization, punctuation, and the like) have been debated for a long, long time, since at least as early as the late 1800s. Melvin J. Hoffman, in his 2008 article *"Echoes of Acrimony: Decades of Grammar Disputes,"* discusses how the arguments that are currently surrounding grammar instruction today parallel the conversations that were occurring over 100 years ago. He concludes:

> From the 1800s to the 2000s, the literature clearly demonstrates that teaching English has never been a comfortable profession ideologically. This is especially the case when questions of grammar are involved.
>
> (Hoffman, 2008, p. 129)

Hoffman provides a number of cases where teachers and researchers out-right reject, or at least call for alternative approaches, to teaching grammar using what we would call a traditional, "drill and (s)kill" method. This can, and often does, include sentence diagramming, conjugating verbs, identifying parts of speech in a piece of writing, or doing any of the myriad types of worksheets or online exercises that one can find by simply searching for "grammar exercises." (Please, don't do that search. Please.)

The debate – often held in the teachers' lounge, department meetings, and occasionally in professional panel conversations – has been vivid. James Kenkel and Robert Yates provide this background in their article *"A Developmental Perspective on the Relationship between Grammar and Text"*:

> from the 1920s through the early 1960s, linguists repeatedly called for English teachers to abandon traditional descriptions in favor of more linguistic ones. The linguistic critique emphasized that descriptions of English offered by traditional grammar have significant shortcomings: its terminology is confusing and more important, its definitions do not reflect what native speakers of the language actually know.
>
> (Kenkel & Yates, 2003, p. 35)

In other words, when we continue to teach students about misplaced modifiers and adverbial clauses, we are missing the bigger picture about why grammar matters: to offer us options – both as speakers and as writers – for creating meaning. Students may (but, most likely will not) memorize these terms for a test, but then have no idea how to apply grammatical knowledge to their own writing. This was the state of the art for decades.

Then, in 1963, the National Council of Teachers of English (NCTE) released a report, *Research in Written Composition*, in which Braddock, Lloyd-Jones, and Schoer state that "[s]tudy after study based on objective testing rather than actual writing confirms that instruction in formal grammar has little or no effect on the quality of student composition" (Braddock, Lloyd-Jones, & Schoer, 1963, p. 37). Despite the definitive nature of this conclusion, the debate around grammar instruction only intensified. Coupled with the rising tide of concern over America's place in the world economy, the ability to read and write became a paramount focus of educational conversations as the baby boom generation came of age.

The debate continued through the 1970s, when Mina Shaughnessy's *Errors and Expectations* set the tone for a (potential) new era, building on the progress of Braddock, Lloyd-Jones, and Schoer. Shaughnessey's masterful insights lead to a simple, powerful claim: teachers "might well begin by trying to understand the logic of their [students'] mistakes in order to determine at what point or points along the developmental path error should or can become a subject for instruction" (Shaughnessy, 1977, p. 13). As a natural part of learning, making errors – and inviting students to analyze these errors – could become a staple of writing instruction. In so doing, a new generation of teachers had the opportunity to reshape the way that grammar was taught and to blend it with good writing instruction.

In the next decade things shifted, but not for the better. The whole language versus phonics debate in reading also carried over into the world of writing. Researchers and teachers drew more lines in the sand while the national conversation around education hardened, too. Anyone familiar with American education since the 1980s is likely very familiar with, arguably, the single most influential education report ever released: *A Nation at Risk* (National Commission on Excellence in Education, 1983). Looking at this report from a 30+ year vantage point, it is sometimes difficult to fully comprehend what this particular document did to shape the course of American schooling: new standards and new tests; the groundwork for school choice and charters; an attempt to get American schools "back to basics" with all the hyperbole of Cold War politics throughout.

While there isn't much in that report that discusses the teaching of writing in particular, one "indicator of risk" stated the challenge in (vague) economic terms:

> Business and military leaders complain that they are required to spend
> millions of dollars on costly remedial education and training programs
> in such basic skills as reading, writing, spelling, and computation.
>
> (*A Nation At Risk*, Online)

Something, of course, needed to be done. Calls for increased accountability through rigorous standards and regular testing led, paradoxically, to teaching that made grammar even more mundane. Countless curricular documents, textbooks, and tests led students to understand the parts of speech, the function of conjunctions, and the difference between "there," "their," and "they're." Yet, did grammar instruction really improve?

According to George Hillocks' seminal work, *Research on Written Composition: New Directions for Teaching* (1986) – published just three years after *A Nation at Risk* – his short answer was "no." His blunt assessment based on a meta-analysis of previous studies made things pretty clear: "The study of traditional school grammar (i.e., the definition of parts of speech, the parsing of sentences, etc.) has no effect on raising the quality of student writing" (p. 248).

These shared ideals were reiterated when NCTE passed a resolution – the "Resolution on Grammar Exercises to Teach Speaking and Writing" (1985) – which noted

> that the use of isolated grammar and usage exercises not supported by theory and research is a deterrent to the improvement of students' speaking and writing and that, in order to improve both of these, class time at all levels must be devoted to opportunities for meaningful listening, speaking, reading, and writing.
>
> (NCTE, Online)

Thus, the battle between idealistic rhetoric and shifting national priorities came about in stark contrast to what researchers and professional organizations were arguing for when it came to the teaching of grammar: doubling down on rote instruction would not do much good. Yet, as children of the 80s and 90s, both Troy and I recall many worksheets and grammar drills in our elementary and middle school days, even the diagramming of sentences. Our guess is that many readers of this book will remember similar experiences.

Still, during that same time period, Constance Weaver championed the cause of teaching grammar in context. With her books *Grammar for Teachers* (1979) and, nearly two decades later, *Teaching Grammar in Context* (1996), Weaver furthered the ideas about isolated grammar instruction as ineffective, noting twelve reasons why teachers continue to teach grammar, despite overwhelming evidence that it is unproductive. Included in her list, paraphrased here from pages 23–25, are the following reasons why some teachers continue to teach grammar in isolated ways:

1. Teachers see that knowledge of grammar is deemed important from a behaviorist perspective of teaching and learning, where more grammar practice equals more learning.
2. Teachers simply do not believe the research about the ineffective practices, as reported by Hillocks, Braddock, Lloyd-Jones, and Schoer, and others.
3. Teachers genuinely believe that the study of grammar is engaging in and of itself, and students would find it so as well.
4. Teachers assume that knowledge of grammar will lead to better reading comprehension and written compositions through conscious awareness rather than contextual practice.
5. Teachers believe that good readers and writers intuitively know (or must learn) grammar, so all students would become more literate with grammar study.

6. On a practical level, it is easy to assign and grade grammar exercises.
7. At the very least, grammar study "does no harm," so it is OK to teach grammar.
8. Curricular requirements and expectations related to grammar were increasing, as noted above.
9. The fear of accountability in the "Nation at Risk" era became more real (and, of course, Weaver was writing well before the era of No Child Left Behind, Race to the Top, or the Every Student Succeeds Act).
10. Teachers might fear parents who demand grammar instruction.
11. Teachers' own school experience included grammar instruction, so their children's schooling should, too.
12. They simply don't know that grammar concepts can be applied to writing "without formal study of grammar as a system."

So, this is where the great grammar debate led us, from the dawn of the twentieth century to the turn of the millennium. These debates among scholars, educators, parents, and policymakers, of course, left collateral damage in the form of children who struggled to learn grammar in a school context that either embraced the role of rote memorization, or embraced a benign neglect by misinterpreting the call to teach grammar in context and, sadly, did not teach it at all.

A brief anecdote from Troy's daughters illustrates this point. The two of them, each enrolled in French (one in eighth grade this year, the other in ninth), were recently having a breakfast table debate about conjugating verbs. The topic: why do we have to learn how to do this in French? We never conjugate verbs in English! In fact, they even asked their dear old dad, the English professor, an earnest question: "Do we even conjugate verbs in English, or is it something that only happens in French and Spanish?" Troy admits that he is no linguist by training, but even a quick Google search on "conjugate English verbs" yields 1.7 million results. Yet, his daughters had never even heard the term in the context of English instruction, nor made the connection on their own.

We have done our students a disservice when it comes to teaching grammar. Let's catch up to the current debate by pushing forward just a bit to the No Child Left Behind (NCLB) era, and watch as history takes another turn.

The Great Grammar Debate, Part 2: 100 Years and Counting

At risk of making this history just a bit too boring, or unpalatable, we turn for just a moment to the changes that happened in the 2000s. The NCLB testing regime became legend in that era, and the effects are still being felt even as we begin to adopt the new approach from the Every Student Succeeds Act (ESSA). While many education advocates and historians can make much more nuanced arguments about the entire era (notably, Alfie Kohn, Diane Ravitch, David Berliner, and Stephen Krashen), suffice it to say that a deep reliance on testing guided the principles of accountability, and that sticks were used with much more frequency than carrots. Thus, grammar took renewed focus in the language section of many tests, and students, most often, were asked to identify errors in existing pieces of writing (or, to identify if it was error-free). Grammar instruction became less about filling in multiple branches in sentence trees and more about multiple choices on bubble sheets.

This, of course, led to a renewed focus on teaching grammar, with the 12 myths that Weaver outlined above even more prominent than before. NCLB era reforms reinforced these myths. Hillocks' and Weaver's work – to the extent it possibly could in the face of NCLB era reforms – guided the teaching of grammar for more than a generation, through the 1980s and 90s. Even though the research and implications for practice were not often implemented in the classroom, the approaches that Hillocks, Weaver, and others advocated for were reaffirmed in 2002 by NCTE's position statement on grammar. One could read this entire statement as an anti-grammar rant, a way to excuse oneself from teaching grammar in any substantive manner. However, NCTE reminds teachers that we should not ignore grammar, noting that

> Students find grammar most interesting when they apply it to authentic texts. Try using texts of different kinds, such as newspapers and the students' own writing, as sources for grammar examples and exercises.
>
> (NCTE's Assembly for the Teaching of English Grammar, 2002, Online)

More importantly, Weaver's work – as well as the title of her 1996 book – suggested that we try approaching grammar instruction in the context of writing. And, more importantly, we see one of her guidelines for teaching grammar, her calls to action, as one guiding purpose for our book. Weaver suggests that one "[b]ecome[s] a teacher-researcher to determine the effects of your teaching of selected aspects of grammar on your students' study of grammar as an object of inquiry and discovery" (p. 146, emphasis in original).

We are thankful that a number of new voices seemed to be responding to this call for an integrated approach, even while NCLB era reforms pushed us toward more rote instruction. Harry Noden's *Image Grammar* (1999, 2011) sought to incorporate these authentic texts in order to develop "[t]he qualities of a writer's images – the details, colors, shapes, movement – [that] derive from visual perception" (p. 3). Noden argues that student writers learn how to add details, like brushstrokes, through elements such as the use of specific verbs and adjectives, as well as literary devices and grammatical structures such as parallel construction, past participial phrases, and hyperbole, among dozens of others. Using these techniques, he believes, will help students develop a toolbox of "image grammar," defined as "a rhetoric of writing techniques that provides writers with artistic grammatical options" (p. 2).

Similarly, and from a distinct writing workshop perspective, Jeff Anderson led the integrated approach with his breakout titles *Mechanically Inclined: Building Grammar, Usage, and Style into Writer's Workshop* (2005) and *Everyday Editing: Inviting Students to Develop Skill and Craft in Writer's Workshop* (2007). The essence of Anderson's approach, in his own words, is that "[g]rammar and mechanics are not rules to be mastered as much as tools to serve a writer in creating a text readers will understand" (p. 5). His books, including his recent co-authored *Revision Decisions: Talking Through Sentences and Beyond* (2014) continues in this same vein, noting that "[s]tudents need to know that it is in the reshaping and re-tweaking – in the redrafting – that we find what's clearer, deeper, and more eloquent" in their writing (Anderson and Dean, 2014, 17). Grammar study, for teacher-writers such as Noden and Anderson, is a tool to create better writers and, in turn, better writing.

While not taking quite the same approach, Don Killgallon reinvigorated the method of sentence composing through a series of books in the late 1990s and into the 2000s. Originally introduced by Frank O'Hare in 1973 through the NCTE research report series, sentence combining is described as "a type of pedagogy involving extensive, sequenced practice of specially formulated print-based exercises through which a student is said to acquire dexterity in writing complex sentences" (1973, p. v). Killgallon's work has stretched from *Sentence Composing for Middle School: A Worktext on Sentence Variety and Maturity* (Killgallon, 1997) into a string of texts for elementary, middle, and high school teachers and students, with his most recent work that invites students to imitate authors' style when writing paragraphs (Killgallon, 1998; Killgallon & Killgallon, 2000, 2012, 2013, 2014).

Just as a more integrated approach to grammar had found a place in the professional discourse about teaching, in 2007, Graham and Perrin then released another meta-analysis in the *Writing Next* report to solidify this importance of this idea. Of all the strategies that could be used to effectively teach writing, including a process writing approach, Graham and Perin argue that isolated grammar instruction was not one of them. They discovered, in fact, that:

Grammar instruction in the studies reviewed involved the explicit and systematic teaching of the parts of speech and structure of sentences. The meta-analysis found an effect for this type of instruction for students across the full range of ability, but surprisingly, this effect was negative. This negative effect was small, but it was statistically significant, indicating that traditional grammar instruction is unlikely to help improve the quality of students' writing.

(Graham & Perin, 2007, p. 21)

Confirming what Hillocks had discovered two decades previous and reaffirming the call for a more integrated approach, Graham and Perrin's report came out just a few years before the Common Core hit the scene. Their conclusion was that "[o]verall, the findings on grammar instruction suggest that, although teaching grammar is important, alternative procedures, such as sentence combining, are more effective than traditional approaches for improving the quality of students' writing" (Graham & Perin, 2007, p. 21).

Other teacher-writers have followed suit with a more integrated approach, especially in recent years, when a look at NCTE, Heinemann, Stenhouse, or any other major publisher's catalog would reveal titles such as:

◆ *Grammar Alive!: A Guide for Teachers* by Brock Haussamen (2003)
◆ *Getting It Right: Fresh Approaches to Teaching Grammar, Usage, and Correctness* by Smith and Wilhelm (2007)
◆ *Getting Grammar: 150 New Ways to Teach an Old Subject* by Donna Topping (2006)
◆ *Teaching Grammar: What Really Works* by Benjamin and Berger (2010)
◆ *Grammar Keepers: Lessons That Tackle Students' Most Persistent Problems Once and for All, Grades 4-12* by Gretchen Bernabei (2015)

Clearly, grammar is still a pertinent topic in the professional literature. Moreover, these titles share a similar, obvious theme: teachers need to make grammar more interesting so students will find the value in it, will want to learn it, and will want to use various techniques in their own writing. For instance, Sandra Wilde hopes in *Funner Grammar* that

this book will inspire you to realize that what we should be helping kids to learn about isn't traditional grammar, but fresh, new grammar, all the strange and wonderful knowledge and information about language that makes it as fun as any other human topic to learn about.

(Wilde, 2012, p. 3)

Similarly, Amy Benjamin with Tom Olivia in *Engaging Grammar* (2007) suggest that they would "like to see you and your students take risks, wrestle with uncertainties, argue over changing rules, splash around in the fun of language" (p. xiii). In contrast to the formulaic workbooks of old, authors like Wilde, Benjamin, Olivia and others acknowledge the distinct possibilities that grammar can play in the lives of writers.

So, in this brief historical summary, it is evident that for more than 100 years, English teachers and researchers have been discussing and arguing for what is the best way to reach our students when it comes to grammar instruction. And, from our individual experiences (Jeremy as a middle school teacher, and Troy as a former middle school teacher and now as a teacher educator who works with in-service and pre-service teachers) to large-scale research analyses, we as a field know that teaching grammar in the context of writing comes out the winner.

The bottom line, therefore, is this: the teaching of grammar is not a separate entity, taught in isolation from writing overall. To have any demonstrable effect on students' abilities as writers, grammar instruction must be integrated.

As we examine student writing, it is important to closely look at what students are struggling with and essentially turn those struggles into teaching moments. These moments are opportunities for mini lessons and authentic discussions encouraging students to learn and apply the elements of good writing. And, this has come into even sharper focus now that the Common Core Standards have begun to shape curriculum and instruction.

The Great Grammar Debate, Part 3: Here Comes the Common Core

Now, with the advent of the Common Core and other state-level standards, we are all faced with a (re)new(ed) focus on the teaching of language and, in particular, the teaching of grammar. As the original Common Core documentation noted,

> Grammar and usage development in children and in adults rarely follows a linear path. Native speakers and language learners often begin making new errors and seem to lose their mastery of particular grammatical structures or print conventions as they learn new, more complex grammatical structures or new usages of English. These errors are often signs of language development as learners synthesize new grammatical and usage knowledge with their current knowledge.

Thus, students will often need to return to the same grammar topic in greater complexity as they move through K–12 schooling and as they increase the range and complexity of the texts and communicative contexts in which they read and write.

(Common Core State Standards Initiative, 2010, Appendix A, p. 28)

This is encouraging. We hear echoes of Shaughnessy in the phrase "errors are often signs of language development" and noting that rote memorization isn't enough when we hear that "students will often need to return to the same grammar topic in greater complexity as they move through K–12 schooling." Perhaps . . . just perhaps . . . we are now moving in the right direction. While the Common Core ELA standards are still open to a great deal of debate and derision (for example, Shannon, 2013), it is clear that they take a more nuanced look at language development, the role of the individual student, and the ways in which writing could be taught.

If we dig deeper, it is notable that the CCSS themselves never use the term "grammar." Instead, what has been traditionally labeled "grammar" can now be found in the "language" standards. Within those standards, students are expected to gain command of the conventions of Standard English, show their knowledge of language and its conventions when reading, writing, speaking, and listening.

First, there are language standards at every grade. For instance, in seventh grade, students are expected to know – and be able to use – simple, compound, and complex sentence structures, misplaced and dangling modifiers, capitalization, coordinate and non-coordinate adjectives, and spelling. Any English teacher who ever talks to his or her colleagues knows that getting student writers to use these skills – as well as the additional standards for hyphens and spelling conventions – is still a challenge. The CCSS hasn't changed that.

Furthermore, vocabulary is highlighted and stressed within the language standards. An accompanying document, "Key Shifts in English Language Arts" describes this goal:

Closely related to text complexity and inextricably connected to reading comprehension is a focus on academic vocabulary: words that appear in a variety of content areas (such as ignite and commit). The standards call for students to grow their vocabularies through a mix of conversation, direct instruction, and reading. They ask students to determine word meanings, appreciate the nuances of words, and steadily expand their range of words and phrases. Vocabulary and conventions are treated in their own strand not because skills in these areas should be handled in isolation, but because their use extends across reading, writing, speaking, and listening.

("Key Shifts in English Language Arts – Common
Core State Standards Initiative," Online)

As we have for decades, teachers and researchers continue to explore what it means to teach grammar, but they do so now with the recursive, progressive manner of language learning in mind. For instance, Amy Benjamin and Joan Berger, in *Teaching Grammar: What Really Works*, state their approach clearly: "We believe it's possible to teach grammar using contemporary methods that result in durable learning" (2010, p. xi). They go on to describe a variety of teaching strategies such as integrating visual media, using hands-on activities, bringing in elements of rhythm, inviting students to play with language, employing logic and reasoning, and searching for patterns.

Sean Ruday, in his book *The Common Core Grammar Toolkit: Using Mentor Texts to Teach the Language Standards in Grades 6-8*, speaks to the purposes of learning grammar:

> I emphasize the relationship between grammatical concepts and tools. An effective writer uses each grammatical concept purposefully, just as a skilled craftsperson uses a tool with a clear understanding of why he or she is using it.
>
> (Ruday, 2014, p. xiii)

Ruday echoes the authors that we saw take this more integrated approach in the 2000s and continues to move the teaching and learning of grammar forward in our modern era. The Common Core has, indeed, renewed our profession's attention on teaching in ways that are both engaging and practical. We appreciate how our colleagues are taking up the challenge of teaching the new language standards in engaging ways.

However, there is a noticeable gap – technology does not appear to be integrated into any of these approaches, at least not in substantive ways. But, when we take an even closer look at the Common Core State Standards (CCSS), there is both an emphasis on grammar instruction as well as an emphasis on the use of technology, a topic we will explore more in Chapter 2. Thus, bridging this gap is the challenge that I took on as Troy and I began our collaboration, and it forms the basis for the rest of this book.

Rethinking Grammar Instruction in a Single Year: A Guide to the Rest of the Book

It is within this context that I began the 2015–16 school year with a renewed focus on the teaching of grammar. I know that I can't teach students everything about reading and writing in just one year, nor should I have to. Yet, I know that we have a great deal of work to do, and I need to engage them through immersive language instruction. So, just like I did in *Create, Compose, Connect!* (2014), I wanted to take on the role of teacher-researcher. Thus, Troy and I began writing this book together, in our single voice, in August of 2015 as I tried to rethink grammar instruction in my classroom.

Though I know that not every one of my students are going to write for a living, they still need to learn how to write, and I feel it is imperative to continue meeting my students where they are today with technology and the way they learn, apply, and retain information. Again, I work diligently to make sure that I don't use technology just as a hook; if they do become more engaged or motivated, then the use of technology is an added perk. Instead, I have willingly taken new approaches to teaching grammar by using tools such as Google Docs, Twitter, and screen captures to help my students see that grammar matters for them as writers, and for their readers, too.

Our hope for this book is that you find a juicy nugget, or an "A-ha!" moment that you can take back into your classroom to use. This book is designed to bounce around and find ideas that you can implement into your daily or weekly writing lessons with your students. Throughout the book, Troy and I have worked together to show you that there can be purposeful ways to use technology when it comes to grammar instruction and the concerns that we have with our students when teaching grammar. In addition, we have a wiki page called textingtoteaching.wikispaces.com that accompanies the book where you can find additional resources. In addition, there will be student examples on the companion wiki of a more complete nature that my students have done. So, without further delay, here is our path for the rest of this journey.

Chapter 2 – An Approach to Teaching Grammar with Digital Tools

In a world full of digital tools, there are many programs, websites, and apps that can be used to engage students in grammar lessons and units, but only when done with intention. This chapter will explore the different tools that not only students can use as resources to help improve their use of grammar, but will focus on specific tools teachers can access to help guide instruction and engage students. From online tools, mobile apps, and apps on the iPad, there are many possibilities with the digital tools that are available.

When considering any of these tools alongside the Triple E Framework by Liz Kolb (2011) – which will be described in this chapter and will be explained in more detail throughout the book – it is important to think about what these tools allow students and teachers to do with grammar instruction that pencil and paper simply cannot. For instance, we can substitute Twitter into our instruction and students can have access to multiple examples in and out of school, and then take Twitter and grammar further by having a Twitter chat about the use of a grammar skill. But, the focus must remain on the teaching . . . not just a conversation about "texting" lingo or the technology itself.

Chapter 3 – Learning the Parts of Speech with Flipped Lessons

As a way to make the study of parts of speech more useful for students and to help create more class time for curriculum and developing enriched discussions, one of the ideas that will be discussed in this chapter will be how flipping grammar instruction has allowed me to create fun and engaging lessons around parts of speech that have led students to apply what they learn from my videos to their daily reading and writing. Throughout the chapter, the process of flipping my grammar instruction will be discussed along with other digital activities that can be completed after students watch instructional videos. When connecting with the Triple E Framework, classroom instruction is driven by making students more active learners and technology gives them opportunities to develop more sophisticated understandings of the content being presented. Furthermore, the chapter will explore digital tools that teachers can use to create flipped instruction in their classroom.

Chapter 4 – Learning Sentence Style with Formal and Informal Writing

One of the possible activities that students can complete each week that is authentic and applicable is a specific revision task. For my students, I provide a template and a very short video through a shared folder on Google Drive along with a sentence or clause that contains a new grammar rule. Working in groups of no more than three people, each small group can work collaboratively and has one week to fill in the template. The template contains a spot for Twitter, Facebook, Instagram, email, and a text message. Each student is responsible for filling out the template along with their name, the rule being learned, and what the rule is in their own words. Students will not be given the grammatical rule right away. The idea is for students to try and discover the rule for themselves through inquiry and apply it to how it could be used across multiple platforms in and out of the classroom. Furthermore, it is one example where the Triple E Framework will allow students to specifically bridge the gap between what they do in school and their everyday lives and in addition, students are learning to understand different writing arenas where they wouldn't be able to with traditional instruction, all while applying grammar skills to what they write. This chapter documents the way that I scaffold this process with my students.

Chapter 5 – Enlivening Vocabulary

Ahh, yes, spelling and vocabulary! A teacher with all the enthusiasm in the world couldn't make these two areas of grammar instruction more engaging for students. However, making real-world connections by having students take their smartphones and have them record how they would use new vocabulary and spelling can help them to understand real-world applications. In addition, students can take their digital devices and find different places, both inside and outside of school, where new words they have learned are being used. When students find these places they may take pictures or create videos with available tools and apps. Again, this chapter will draw on the Triple E Framework in terms of students using tools such as cellphones to help show what they have mastered and break down the walls of school.

Chapter 6 – Mastering Mechanics: Capitalization and Punctuation

When it comes to capitalization and punctuation, these two aspects of grammar instruction can be the most frustrating for teachers, especially at the secondary level when students should know how to use these skills properly. Yet, is this just a formality? Teachers often blame "text speak" for these two commonly misused skills. However, through the use of text messages, social media posts, and the use of Google Documents, students can collaborate and reflect on how changing punctuation and using capitalization where necessary can change the tone and voice in writing. In addition, students can learn to differentiate between formal and informal writing while learning how to code switch effectively. Students can use other less well-known forms of punctuation to really enhance their writing style. For instance, they often only teach colons, semicolons, and dashes in a brief manner at the middle school grades, yet when done well, we can help students really develop a sense of style.

Chapter 7 – Assessing Grammar in a Digital Age

While thinking about how grammar instruction can be delivered to students in a digital world – and why it is important to consider grammar as a part of education today – students will be applying what they have learned about grammar and sentence construction through cross-curricular projects such as our Civil War Day Research Paper (social studies) and our Salmon in the Classroom Project (science and math). By extending what they have learned in other content areas, students will become better writers (and, we hope, more teachers will benefit from the quality of writing that students will complete for them). Also, students see value in learning the grammar skills placed before them and not just something they have to memorize for a week and then move on to something new. Furthermore, by utilizing technology and the digital spaces students interact in, they are more likely to be engaged in the learning process and learn how to differentiate between their digital world and their academic world.

Given the history of grammar instruction, the debate for both *how* to teach grammar as well as *what* to teach in relation to grammar is going to continue. What works for one school or for one teacher may not work exactly the same way for another, so customizing ideas to meet your students' needs is certainly fine. But, the evidence is clear: we cannot rely on rote memorization and grammar drills. These approaches simply do not work. What we do know is that the landscape is continuing to change and as educators, we need to meet our students where they are and help them to use technology in meaningful ways. We hope that you can adapt some of these ideas as you begin to think about what it means to teach grammar in a digital age.

2

An Approach to Teaching Grammar with Digital Tools

Teaching continues to be my vocation, and my avocation. I have worked each year to get just a little better. And, as I described in *Create, Compose, Connect!*, by the 2010–11 school year, I had integrated technology into many of my lessons . . . with the distinct exception of grammar.

First, a quick rewind to my life before 2010. Quite honestly, I was ready to give up on teaching at the middle school level. I was starting to think about going back to the elementary level. A colleague had encouraged me to attend the Summer Institute hosted by the Chippewa River Writing Project, a satellite site of the National Writing Project at Central Michigan University. When I was accepted, little did I know that after the four weeks of intensive writing and immersive professional development with Troy and about 20 other colleagues, I would go back into my classroom and completely overhaul the way I taught writing. It was the best professional development that I have ever been a part of in my teaching career.

After completing the Summer Institute for the Chippewa River Writing Project in 2010, and reading *The Digital Writing Workshop* (2009) by Troy, much of my approach about how I was going to engage my students in my language arts class had changed. In particular, many of my ideas about teaching language arts with technology had changed, and I was pleased at the growth my students showed. That's what led to *Create, Compose, Connect!*, where I admitted that, at one time, I was part of the "cell phone brigade" in my building. Contrast that with what I learned in the writing project, and I began to see that "inviting my students to use their digital devices isn't a novelty; it's a necessity" (Hyler and Hicks, p. 2).

Though I changed many aspects of my teaching that year, grammar instruction stagnated. Up to this point, it had been mostly "drill and kill" where my students would get out battered grammar books and then, begrudgingly, get to work. As I mentioned in *Create, Compose, Connect!*, I had not been a big fan of allowing students to use personal mobile devices in my classroom. Due to my lack of knowledge about the available tools and having not had the experience of classroom-based research, I was under the impression that students were being distracted by the technology that they were using. I'm glad that all changed. But, as I noted above, grammar instruction was stuck. I needed to think about how to take a similar approach and ways to make it happen with grammar instruction.

There is ample evidence that technology has changed our language, and will continue to do so in the future. Graham and Perrin argue that "The explosion of electronic and wireless communication in everyday life brings writing skills into play as never before" (2007, p. 8), and instantaneous publishing opportunities mean that the need for grammar instruction plays out in students' public writing. As we have for generations, teachers today struggle with students not being able to differentiate between formal and non-formal writing. However, contrary to what many people believe, texting and technology alone are not to blame for the woes we may face when it comes to evaluating student writing that may be riddled with "text speak" language.

Before I started doing more research on the issue, I assumed that students were developing some very poor habits while texting and using social media sites such as Facebook and Twitter. For instance, students were still not capitalizing the "I's" in their writing, or they were using the letter "u" in place of the word "you." Anyone who is a parent will recognize this in their child's writing, and perhaps even in their own! On a surface level, these kind of errors will drive an English teacher nuts, and I wanted to figure out how to fix them.

Other issues included students failing to compose the variety of sentences that are needed throughout their writing. I have found it very difficult for students to retain what parts make up the various types of sentences and effectively use the different types of sentences – compound, complex, and compound-complex – in their own writing. This is difficult enough when asking them to compose sentences on paper or with a word processor. When I saw the types of sentences that most students were composing using social media, however, my inner grammarian started going crazy again.

Also, my students were struggling with using past and present tense verbs correctly, not to mention subject-verb agreement. For any given writing assignment I would collect from one class of students, I would typically find that nearly half of them would still have these types of errors, even after we had proofread. I felt the need – and the responsibility – to help my students develop writing habits that would bring them success in a digital world. However, even after implementing technology into my lessons and teaching my students new digital tools such as Google Docs, they were still struggling with grammar mistakes. Even those that used a grammar checker didn't fully understand why certain corrections were being suggested.

I was beginning to believe it was a retention problem and that students' writing habits were indeed being inhibited by their technology use; more specifically, I assumed that it was from their laziness when texting and using social media. The struggle wasn't just in my own classroom; other teachers in my department were experiencing the same issues, and stories in the popular media were confirming our suspicions. For example, a Penn State article in July 2012 titled "No LOL matter: Tween texting may lead to poor grammar skills," proclaims that students who use "text speak" to communicate quickly with their friends performed more poorly on tests (Swayne & Messer). Another article by *The Telegraph* titled "Texting is fostering bad grammar and spelling, researchers claim" discusses the idea that the more students text, the worse they do on tests. It seems that technology – and the more that students use it – causes students to have poorer writing skills (The Telegraph, 2012).

In conversations with Troy, colleagues at our writing project, and within the broader community of teachers in my personal learning network (PLN), I suspected that something else had to be at play. Troy and I thought about the work that the many researchers and teachers we discussed in Chapter 1 had done over many, many decades. Mina Shaughnessy's work has been an influence on Troy, and we discussed the ways in which students were using the expectations of an informal, spoken-language structure for their writing even when the audience and purpose changed. Rather than getting more and more frustrated with my students, Troy and I began to look for answers, as well as ways to adapt my instruction.

So, what does research say about digital devices, "text speak," and the effects on our students? Despite our common-sense response that technology is ruining our language, the answers for linguists and other literacy researchers may surprise you . . . they certainly surprised me.

What the Research Says: The (Non) Effects of Text Speak

As I continued to do research and talk with colleagues, I discovered that research was yielding answers that did not align to my preconceived explanation. In fact, I found many articles where researchers claimed texting was not to blame. As is often the case with many elements of our common-sense thinking, I began questioning my own assumptions about why students would carry over "text speak" into their writing. Before I describe that shift in my own thinking, here is some of what we found as Troy and I delved into the research.

In his aptly titled 2006 article from the *Journal of Computer-Mediated Communication*, "From Statistical Panic to Moral Panic: The Metadiscursive Construction and Popular Exaggeration of New Media Language in the Print Media," Thurlow analyzes 101 media reports from 2001 to 2005, all related to the use of text speak. From his critical look at these reports, he draws one major conclusion:

> [D]espite the media headlines that suggest that use of text speak in written assignments is becoming commonplace, there is no sound empirical evidence that textisms are, in fact, surfacing in students' formal written communication.
>
> (Thurlow, 2006, paraphrased in Drouin and Davis, 2009, p. 50)

A few short years later, Drouin and Davis echo this point in their analysis of 80 college students, about half of whom often used text speak and half who did not. Summarizing their findings in the abstract for their article in *The Journal of Literacy Research*, these authors note that:

> [T]here were no significant differences between the two groups in standardized literacy scores or misspellings of common text speak words.
>
> (2009, p. 50)

All of this work showed that, indeed, students in our modern era – much like the ones that Shaughnessy had studied – were apt to make errors occasionally, but that often depended on context. In other words, students were able to move back and forth between formal and informal language when they made a conscious effort.

Additionally, I was introduced to the work of Kristen Hawley Turner, a professor of English Education and Contemporary Literacies, whose research on "digitalk" gave me new insights into the socio-linguistic processes unfolding in my students' speech and writing, in school and out. She argues that

> In the digital world adolescents choose the communities to which they belong; they decide to what extent they will engage in the norms of those communities; they determine the level of language play that will mark their individual identities. In school, however, this power to choose often does not exist, and tasks assigned have little value to teens beyond the assessment.
>
> (2012, p. 40)

She describes how "digitalk," like slang or other linguistic markers, has helped students develop their own community and as teachers we need to embrace what students are engaged in when it comes to their world. Turner found that students were able to successfully code switch – that is, they could move quickly and fluently between academic and social discourse. More importantly, when "primary discourses include digitalk, teens have the space and the tools to communicate in ways that distinguish their being-doing-valuing systems and mark their membership to specific communities" (Turner, Abrams, Katíc, & Donovan, 2014, p. 160).

In short, the few studies that had been done disproved the popular notion that texting actually decreased students' grammar skills. To put it another way . . . research says that "text speak" or "digitalk" is not ruining our children's grammar. OMG!

This was good news, but I still wasn't satisfied. I wanted to better understand how, exactly, technology affects students' language arts skills and, in the past two years, my attention has turned to thinking about adding grammar instruction similar to the transformational approaches by teachers such as Jeff Anderson, Sean Ruday, Rebecca Wheeler and others, with the added twist that I bring a more intentional focus on using technology. In doing so, I could more clearly help my students understand what it means to accomplish a variety of writing tasks. They may combine sentences, adjust their words or phrasing, or simply learn how to separate items into a list with commas. Using technology, we have the opportunity to explore our own writing process and use grammatical resources to make our writing better.

Thus, as we did in *Create, Compose, Connect!*, Troy and I want to use this book as an opportunity to think about how technology can enhance writing instruction. Smart grammar instruction – coupled with smart uses of technology – will help improve students' understanding of how to use various sentence patterns, phrases, punctuation, and other stylistic techniques in their own writing, which can make them the astute writers we want them to become. Furthermore, it can help them retain the skills and concepts because they are being taught with tools that they themselves are familiar with.

In order to address our particular concerns about teaching grammar in the digital age, we begin with an assumption that most students in today's classroom have devices in their pockets or available to them at school. While we know that there are still exceptions to this rule, and that the digital divide is real, the simple fact is that more teens have mobile devices or adequate access at school than ever before. Rather than being fancy tools for texting and social media, Troy and I believe that we, as educators and role models, can help students to use these devices in productive, thoughtful ways to become better writers.

As we demonstrated in Chapter 1, we can argue convincingly that good grammar instruction does not consist of teaching grammar independently or as a separate subject. More effective instruction involves students looking at grammar within the context of their writing and also seeing the moves other writers make through mentor texts. Then, students take what they have learned and experiment with those moves themselves within their own writing. To accomplish these goals, we need to redefine grammar instruction in a digital age, a task we turn to next, and use a new framework for thinking about technology integration, Liz Kolb's Triple E.

Redefining Grammar Instruction in a Digital Age

Noting the many studies above that have already disproven the idea that technology is ruining students' grammar, we need to recognize that there are no good reasons to blame their phones, tablets, and computers. The kids are, indeed, all right. Technology is not destroying our children.

Thus, this leads to a more important question, one that all of us as users of the English language and as ELA teachers really need to pause to ask: what does a grammatically astute writer look and act like in the digital world?

When Troy and I began to look for answers to this question, one immediate challenge is that grammar and technology are often equated to the use of spelling and grammar checking tools, or using online games to teach grammatical concepts. A quick search of "grammar technology" in December of 2015 yielded over 71 million hits, and the top results led to headlines such as "Practice Grammar With Technology" or "7 Great Grammar Sites for Teachers and Students." (See, we said not to search for this stuff!)

And, while we can empathize with the teacher who is struggling to make a lesson plan for tomorrow, it is still our responsibility as educators to deliver grammar instruction effectively and not just use technology for the sake of using it; instead, we can help students use technology in meaningful and effective ways that can empower them to become better writers.

So, to see them as competent and creative writers who can use technology, let's turn back to the *Writing Next* report to lay the foundation for my approach to teaching grammar with technology.

> Most contexts of life (school, the workplace, and the community) call for some level of writing skill, and each context makes overlapping, but not identical, demands. Proficient writers can adapt their writing flexibly to the context in which it takes place.
>
> (p. 9)

In this quote, we encounter the ideas of "context," "adaptation," and "flexibility." These are, indeed, skills that a good writer must possess, and are similar to the "habits of mind" that the National Writing Project, National Council of Teachers of English, and Council of Writing Program Administrators call for in their *Framework for Success in Postsecondary Writing* (2011). According to these three professional organizations, these habits of mind are "ways of approaching learning that are both intellectual and practical and that will support students' success in a variety of fields and disciplines" and include traits such as curiosity, engagement, and persistence, among others. Again, all are traits that students will need to use as writers of both print and digital texts.

For instance, just today, Troy was carrying on text messaging and chat conversations with a variety of family members, friends, and colleagues. In a conversation with his daughter via smartphone, the abbreviations he used in the text messages were entirely appropriate and, more importantly, appealing to his audience: an eighth grader who is obsessed with selfies, her emoji keyboard, and the avatar creation app Bitmoji. She even replied with a smiling emoji at one point, a huge score for the father of a middle school student. In fact, he's pretty sure his daughter would have laughed at him if he had only used proper English all the time during the chat. Emoticons, sometimes, can convey a great deal of information, especially to a 14-year-old. So, just as we teach students how to switch between formal and informal situations, we must also help them understand how to use "digitalk" in these situations for a variety of home, school, and workplace goals.

In addition to the goal of creating more sophisticated, adaptable writers, there are a variety of reasons that we can think of for teaching grammar with technology. In the spirit of Weaver, who outlined numerous excuses for why teachers may choose *not* to teach grammar in an integrated manner, we use a similar approach here and suggest five reasons why we *should* be teaching grammar in transformative manner, enabled by smart uses of technology:

1. *Standards suggest that we should.* The Common Core State Standards asks us to explore the use of technology within our classrooms. More specifically, within the language standards under Vocabulary Acquisition and use, seventh grade standard L.7.4.C wants students to explore reference materials that are both digital and printed in format. "Consult general and specialized reference materials (e.g., dictionaries, glossaries, thesauruses), both print and digital, to find the pronunciation of a word or determine or clarify its precise meaning or its part of speech" (Corestandards.org).

   Additionally, some of the writing standards (where students will use the language skills) shows evidence technology should play a role in what students are doing and how they learn. For instance, the seventh grade writing standard for producing and distributing writing, standard W.7.6, clearly states students should use technology to help produce and publish their writing. "Use technology, including the Internet, to produce and publish writing and link to and cite sources as well as to interact and collaborate with others, including linking to and citing sources" (Corestandards.org).

   We can't ignore the fact that our curriculum asks us to implement technology into our lessons and units. Though it doesn't state specifically how we are to go about implementing it, we at least have some general guidance.

2. *Organization is (or, at least could be) easier in digital spaces.* With tools such as Google Docs and Slides, as well as many other cloud-based services, students can't claim they lost a paper or forgot their work at home or school. There is no excuse for losing it. So, staying organized is as good a reason as any for having students explore grammar with digital tools.

3. *Digital citizenship has become an essential skill.* As mentioned in the International Society for Technology in Education (ISTE) standards for teaching, students should be taught the responsibility of using tools effectively. Teacher standard 4b, where teachers should promote and model digital citizenship, specifically calls for teachers to "address the diverse needs of all learners by using learner-centered strategies providing equitable access to appropriate digital tools and resources"

(iste.org/standards). Showing students how to use language in grammatically-appropriate ways through a variety of technologies is a natural extension of this digital citizenship goal.

4. *Access is improving.* While we know that some students still struggle to get access outside of school, the vast majority are able to get online via broadband, cellular data, or with publicly available Wi-Fi. One of the wonderful features about using technology and implementing it into any classroom is the idea that students can work on their assignments anywhere if they had access to do it: the car, at home, a friend's house, the doctor's office, etc. Also, students can work collaboratively on assignments and technology allows students to be connected to their teachers whenever a question or an issue that may arise. To put it simply, the walls of the classroom no longer restrict student's learning, and language learning is no exception.

5. *Revision matters.* Finally, students do understand the differences between revising and editing, which is crucial for them to become better writers. Technology enables this process. In particular, I use Anderson and Dean's "DRAFT" process from *Revision Decisions: Talking Through Sentences and Beyond* (2014) where they "Delete," "Rearrange," "Add," "Form," and "Talk" as a way to teach revision. My students are able to use these strategies with Google Docs and then reflect on the moves that they made as writers to accomplish their revisions. They can track and reflect upon their revisions, and that process provides many opportunities for thinking about grammar, too.

There are bound to be more items that could be added to the list, yet I will end there for now. For me, as a result of implementing more technology into my own classroom, I can confidently argue that students are more engaged with my lessons and units and my students are retaining more of the grammatical ideas that are being presented to them in middle school. Moreover, students are having deliberate conversations about grammar and how certain skills should be used in their writing. Recently, my students were revising their student choice writing using the DRAFT process by Jeff Anderson and Deborah Dean. I wanted to place my phone down in the middle of the table of this group of students to record them because they were literally having an argument about whether a sentence was a run-on. Believe it or not, my students were in a debate about a semicolon! Those types of conversations give me goose bumps as an educator. Yes, I am a nerd, and I am proud of it!

Earlier, I mentioned that there are many different ways that schools have implemented technology into their school. And, sadly, we know that there are schools who have not implemented much at all. Some teachers may only have one iPad to use in their classroom, but even that can become a learning tool for all. Whatever the situation may be, it is fair to say that teachers of all levels need guidance. Depending on the level of knowledge and what technology is available to teachers, we are continuing to learn next to our students, especially with how to best utilize digital tools and spaces.

One of the best things I have ever done as a teacher is to let my guard down when it came to me thinking I had to be the expert when using a digital tool with my students. Let's face it, as teachers, we don't have time to know the ins and outs of every tool, especially when we pick up that powerful morsel at a conference and we want to implement it right away into our classrooms. What I have found that works well is to set guidelines for students and model for them the features of a tool that you know. At the same time, however, being open and honest with them about what features teachers don't know too well also works. Believe it or not, students may figure things out much faster. It not only saves us time, but the students feel empowered because they taught their teacher something new.

With a device in hand, we have almost arrived at the time to begin thinking about how to utilize technology for grammar instruction. The last part of this chapter is laid out so readers can skip right to their own comfort level and even come back to the chapter later once they feel more comfortable going on to the next level. These are the tools that we will return to again and again throughout the book, so it is worth taking some time to explore them all at some point or another, thinking carefully about how they could enhance instruction. We tried to keep every level of expertise in mind, while also giving readers some tools that are useful to teachers alone, and are not necessarily for students to use. Before we get into the tools, however, we have one more important element to mix into your planning and decision-making about technology: educational technology expert and author, Liz Kolb's Triple E Framework for analyzing technology use in your teaching.

Triple E Framework: Engage, Enhance, Extend

Throwing technology at existing lessons just for the sake of using technology isn't the answer. As educators, we need to think about effective implementation that produces positive learning outcomes for our students and assures there will be achievement. In 2011, University of Michigan professor

Liz Kolb developed the Triple E Framework that addresses that very issue (see www.tripleeframework.com for more details). The framework describes three levels: engagement, enhancement, and extension. Kolb, a former classroom teacher, and as someone who has taught others about educational technology for over a decade, knows that she must provide some kind of framework for teachers as they begin to think about their goals.

What Kolb offers with her framework that other frameworks lack is that it goes beyond just "engaging" the students. As she notes on the Triple E Framework website:

> Engagement is the most basic level of technology integration. Often by putting a piece of technology in front of the students or in their hands, they become interested or "engaged" in the activity. However, we can look a little more deeply at engagement by considering if the technology is not just capturing the interest of the student, but if it is actually engaging them actively in the content (not just the bells and whistles of the software).

As seen in Image 2.1, the framework is designed to work from the bottom where an educator begins thinking about a technology with the "Engage" questions and works towards the top through "Enhance" and "Extend," all the while asking three questions under each category. The framework works through steps that encourage educators to implement technology so students can apply what they are doing beyond the classroom. Furthermore, I think that the framework is simple and easy to follow where others might be difficult to understand, especially to teachers who are just beginning the journey of implementing technology. Overall, I feel this framework fits best into my planning. It allows me to think critically, carefully, and creatively about what I am doing in my classroom, especially when it comes to using technology with the teaching of grammar. And, perhaps most importantly, Kolb's framework can easily be followed and applied to any teaching and technology integration situation.

Not only because we are both fans of the Triple E Framework (and Liz Kolb herself!), both Troy and I encourage teachers to review the website because it is clear, concise, and also includes a form that you can use to evaluate ed-tech tools using the framework. Best of all, Dr. Kolb has made this framework available for teachers to use in a variety of contexts by licensing it under a Creative Commons Attribution Non-Commercial 4.0 International License, so you are free to adapt and remix it in your lessons and professional development sessions.

Now, on to the digital writing tools that I use in my classroom.

Image 2.1 The Triple E Framework by Liz Kolb

Extend	Does the technology create opportunities for students to learn outside of their typical school day?
	Does the technology create a bridge between school learning and everyday life experiences?
	Does the technology allow students to build grit skills, that they can use in their everyday lives?
Enhance	Does the technology tool aid students in developing a more sophisticated understanding of the content
	Does the technology create scaffolds to make it easier to understand concepts or ideas
	Does the technology allow students to demonstrate their understanding of content that they could not do traditionally
Engage	Does the technology allow students to focus on the assignment or activity with less distraction
	Does the technology motivate students to start the learning process
	Does the technology cause a shift in the behaviour of the students, where they move from passive to active learners

Source: Reproduced with permission from www.tripleeframework.com.

Tools of the Trade: Technologies for Digital Grammar Instruction

Choosing the right tools for what you would like to do in your classroom can be challenging. Troy and I feel it is important to consider making a choice on what tool to use while keeping the Triple E Framework in mind as you are choosing the tool. The framework offers a series of questions that can help in making the right decision for what tool works in a given situation. Though all of the questions that are asked are very important, these specific questions resonate with me when I think about the type of digital tools I want to use for my students or with my students when it comes to grammar instruction.

- *Engage*
  - Does the technology motivate students to start the learning process?
- *Enhance*
  - Does the technology create paths for students to demonstrate their understanding of the learning goals in a way that they could not do with traditional tools?

◆ *Extend*

   o Does the technology create a bridge between school learning and everyday life experiences?
   o Does the technology allow students to build skills that they can use in their everyday lives?

Again, the Triple E Framework as a whole is important, but when thinking about grammar skills, I want my students to not only be engaged and motivated, but I want them to have a clear understanding of what is being taught in relation to grammar. In addition, I want them to apply the skills they are learning to everyday life in and out of school, no matter where they are at with their thinking about future schooling or careers.

Each tool has become a foundational part of my digital teaching, and we describe how these tools align with various levels of technology experience: beginner, intermediate, and advanced. The tools in the table below will be mentioned later on in the book as well. There is always the chance that a teacher may be an expert with one technology we list and to be able to use it in many different ways, and we don't categorize in any attempt to offend. Everyone has their own favorites, for sure.

We do, however, want to lay out some potential paths for teachers as they begin to explore technologies that can lead to better grammar instruction, and this seemed to be a logical way to do it. In the "beginner" category, we suggest tools that require little more than an account to sign in, a quick app or browser installation, and not much more. Also, all of these tools are free. Then, in the "intermediate" category, we suggest tools that may take a little more time to install and learn, but are still relatively easy to use for their designed purposes, especially for screen capture or screencasting. Finally, in the "expert" category, we suggest two tools that I have been using to create hybrid, or flipped, lessons.

As a side note, links to these tools – and more examples of how I use them – can also be found on our wiki page that accompanies the book, texting-toteaching.wikispaces.com. We are not going to explain each and every tool in a great deal of detail, partially because the technology is always changing and partially because there are so many good "getting started" type resources on the web. For the moment, we encourage readers to take a look at the lists and explore the programs, apps, and websites that may not be familiar to them.

Beginner: Getting Started with Screen Capture, Screencasting, and Annotation

So, we all have to start someplace when it comes to technology, right? Some of us are more comfortable than others plunging head first into new

Figure 2.1 Beginner Tools for Teaching Grammar with Technology

Tool	Purpose	Set-up	Cost	Link
Google Documents	Create folders and documents for students to have grammar resources for future use.	Students open multiple documents where they have tables that include grammar concept, rule, and examples for students to refer to for later use.	Free with Google Account or Google Apps for Education	google.com/docs/about
Google Slides	Students duplicate pre-made templates to help them investigate grammar rules and where students can learn the difference between formal and informal writing.	Teacher creates social media templates and students make copies to use for group work and individual work.	Free with Google Account or Google Apps for Education	google.com/slides/about
Fake Apple Texting	Students create fake iPhone messages using the website and can demonstrate their use of the different parts of speech and their ability to shift between formal and informal writing spaces.	Students access website on computers and create the fake texts without usernames or passwords. Students must take a screenshot of what they created.	Free	ios7text.com/
Vine	An app to make short six second videos. Students can create short vocabulary videos with the app.	Students can link to an existing Twitter account, otherwise a username and password is required.	Free	vine.co
Fakebook	Great tool for students to practice writing in a space that they typically spend a lot of time in, though it is not real. Can be used for sentence structure.	Students fill in the information on the website and need to take a screenshot of what they do.	Free	classtools.net/FB/home-page
Open Screenshot	Take screenshots of mentor texts for students to highlight grammar concepts and parts of speech writers use. Also, for students to rewrite and rework sentences.	This tool is a Google Chrome App or add-on that can be added to your chrome bar and accessed with your Google account.	Free	openscreenshot.com
Awesome Screenshot	Another screenshot tool that students and teachers can annotate. Screenshots can be uploaded directly to the website.	App can be downloaded on any device and also through your Chrome browser.	Free	awesomescreenshot.com

challenges and implementing the changes necessary to make our students more engaged and more successful with digital tools. In the "beginner" section of Figure 2.1, I focus on seven tools that can be used by both teachers and students.

The tools in the "beginner" tier of the figure are meant for teachers who want simple, yet effective, tools for their students. I also believe they are tools where teachers can learn alongside their students and perhaps figure out some of the basic features together. Students make great teachers, too, when it comes to technology.

Intermediate: Sharing Media and Assessing Students' Understanding

Moving up a level to "intermediate," this next group of tools allow those educators who are a bit more comfortable and confident of implementing technology into their classroom a chance to experiment with not only continuing to break down the walls of the classroom for the students, but also a chance to show students how to use social media in responsible and resourceful ways. In terms of the tool Explain Everything, it is a more complex tool for creating flipped lessons or resource videos for your students. Compared to Snag-It, there are more features than just simply recording a video of a screen or yourself. Though I feel the tools below (Figure 2.2) are not overly-complicated to navigate and use, they do require more time to learn and have more features, so they will take some time to master and implement.

One quick note: Snag-it is not something that is not going to be widely available to all students. With it costing around $50, it is a tool that isn't going used school-wide on student computers. Still, if you are interested in flipping any part of your instruction, especially grammar (Chapter 3), Snag-it is a great beginning tool to record lessons for students to watch and review.

Expert: Producing and Publishing More Enriched Media

"Complicated" can be an intimidating word to some, so I will refrain from using that term and go with "in-depth" as a way to describe the "expert" level! Though the tools are not difficult to learn, they can require more knowledge of all of the features that they offer (Figure 2.3). The first, Touchcast, is free, but they limit your uploads to only one hour, although you can create as many videos as you want. Also, Touchcast is only available to iOS users. Touchcast is not set up to work through a web browser, only through the app. Touchcast could be used by both teachers and students. I can see the

Figure 2.2 Intermediate Tools for Teaching Grammar with Technology

Tool	Purpose	Set-up	Cost	Link
Celly	Celly can be used to help with back channeling conversations and with conversations during class that will take place outside of school about grammar.	Email and password required for to sign up. Teachers create cells for students to participate in class discussions.	Free	cel.ly
Twitter	Students can learn how to use punctuation such as colons and semicolons in sentences due to the 140 character limit. Hashtags can be created for students to utilize for a resource on grammar examples.	Username and password required along with a valid email. Teachers can create hashtags for students to post examples of grammar concepts.	Free	twitter.com
Quizlet	An online tool and app that can be used to create study flashcards for students or by students. Flashcards can be made into online games to help study.	Username and password are required, but a Google account can be used. Students do not need an account to access teacher-created content, just the link. Available as an application also for Apple and Android	Free	quizlet.com
Edpuzzle	A digital tool that can be used to annotate videos, including pre-existing videos. Educators can create discussion points or quizzes for students as they are watching.	Can be used on any device including Apple and Android. Also, it can be used as a Chrome app and a YouTube extension. User needs to create a free account.	Free	edpuzzle. com
Jing	A simple tool to capture short screencasts or single screenshots on your computer with the ability to store them. Short videos can be made with accessible by giving links to students.	Can be downloaded on Mac or PC through the Techsmith website.	Free – with 2GB of free storage of videos every month.	techsmith. com/jing. html
Snag-it	Use to create flipped lessons or to tape lessons that students may have difficulties with. In addition, teachers can use the tool to capture videos for absent students. You could use it to capture your webcam and record the screen as well. One could master this in less than an hour.	Can be downloaded on Mac or PC through the Techsmith website.	$49.95	techsmith. com/snagit. html

Explain Everything	Tool that can be used to annotate and manipulate documents that are useful for grammar instruction.	iPhone or iPad application that can also be used on laptops as well. Download required for use.	$5.99	explain everything. com
Screencastify	This is a plugin that is added to your Chrome extensions which allows screen capturing and is linked to your Google account for easy uploading to YouTube or your Google Drive.	Plugin for Google Chrome. Works well if you have an existing Google account.	There is a free version that allows 10 minutes of recording. The paid version is a one-time payment of about $22 and gives you unlimited space with no watermarks.	screencastify. com

potential for students creating some amazing videos for book trailers and other projects. Touchcast can be a great tool for teachers to create flipped lessons while embedding multiple resources for students to look over while watching the video.

Camtasia, for me, is best described as Snag-it on steroids. It is a tool where you can use video with music, text, pictures, and other neat things like transitions. If you like creating videos and love video production, this is a tool for you and your students. It comes with a bit of a price tag, but is a great program if you plan to create many lessons and want customized editing features. It is available for both Mac and PC computers.

Figure 2.3 Expert Tools for Teaching Grammar with Technology

Tool	Purpose	Set-up	Cost	Link
Touchcast	A more elaborate screencasting tool that can be used to create flipped grammar lessons. Teachers can incorporate links, pictures, sound effects, and resources directly into the videos that are created.	Requires username and password and knowledge of integrating different tools into the screencast.	Free	touchcast.com
Camtasia	This is by far the most advanced tool that is available for screencasting and creating flipped lessons. Camtasia allows more access to editing and integrated music, pictures, and text.	Downloaded onto computer. No username or password required.	$179 PC or $75 Mac (Education price)	techsmith.com/ camtasia.html

And . . . We're Off . . . Ready, Tech, Go!

With the tools in the figures presented earlier, I am really hoping that, as teachers, we can all integrate at least one digital tool into our current grammar lessons or perhaps completely transform how we do things with students when it comes to grammar. Troy and I hope to show you how to do this throughout the book by illustrating our ideas with examples of what I am doing inside my own classroom. We are not asking anyone to become experts with every technology listed here. However, we need to recognize that students engage with technology and media in their daily lives and – while we do not want to simply create "edutainment" or try to engage students in gimmicky ways – we need to take further steps in meeting our students where they are at today.

In terms of the students, I am really hoping – with their abundant access to technology – that they can learn to not only use the tools in responsible and meaningful ways, but they can access resources they have created at any time they may need them. Furthermore, I want my students to have a solid foundation with grammar before they enter high school where they can polish their writing to an even greater extent without having to worry about the basics. No matter what area you feel more comfortable with, these tools can be used in purposeful ways by both teachers and students. These tools will be discussed throughout the book. Feel free to bounce around and see where they are being used!

Once you establish your own area of expertise and comfort, it is also important to think about tools that are easy for your students as well. Oftentimes we can forget about the student because we are trying to learn the tool ourselves. As you consider which level you feel that you are comfortable with, thinking about how the tool can be used to enhance the lessons we are teaching students is more important. We want our students to be engaged, but we don't want to use technology just for the sake of using technology. Students still need to learn the skills, but need to learn how it can be applied in the digital spaces they may occupy. That's where we are heading in the rest of this book, and Chapter 3 discusses multiple ways to teach students parts of speech with flipped lessons.

3

Learning the Parts of Speech with Flipped Lessons

"Who can remind all of us what a pronoun is and how it is used in our writing?" I ask as I look out over my middle school students, waiting for some energetic hands to burst towards the ceiling.

Nothing appears, short of silence and awkward stares at each other as if the answer is going to magically appear on their classmates' foreheads.

"Mr. Hyler, I don't remember what a pronoun is."

"WHAT?" I bellow.

"Isn't it a describing word?" one student blurts out.

I sigh heavily, and they know that they are about to get another lesson on pronouns.

Does this situation sound familiar at all? Well, it seemed to be a re-run in my classroom every year and to be honest, it still can be from time-to-time depending on the conversation that I am having with my students.

Parts of speech are no doubt crucial for students' success as they begin constructing sentences and making their writing not just better, but more powerful. They need to understand something as simple as how words like "cook," "wash," or "rake" can be used as a noun and verb, or how changing the usage can change the meaning of the sentence.

As history has shown (and as we document in Chapter 1), the problem for my students is that the information about nouns, verbs, pronouns, adjectives, adverbs, prepositions, conjunctions, and interjections – don't forget interjections! – is that the information has (most often) not been taught to them in their earlier education in ways that help them truly understand the concept, and therefore they have not internalized it. In the past, I, too, was guilty of teaching students grammar in isolation. I would make students haul their 500-page grammar and writing book back and forth with them every day to class. It was either doing problems out of the book or worksheets I handed them. I was getting to the point that I was tired of teaching parts of speech in isolation and handing them worksheets, too.

I knew I had to change my teaching practices. So, I decided to "flip" parts of my grammar instruction, specifically the ways I taught parts of speech, word choice, and sentence structure. By "flipping," I am referring to the process similar to that which the Flipped Learning Network defines. They state that flipped learning is where direct instruction moves from the group learning space to the individual learning space, and the resulting group space is transformed into a dynamic, interactive learning environment where the educator guides students as they apply concepts and engage creatively in the subject matter (Flipped Learning Network, Online).

Here, I outline some of the reasons why I flip my instruction:

◆ I don't have to spend class time doing mundane worksheets with my students; I post the lesson on Monday, and they work at their own pace over the week.

◆ By the time that they get to Friday, our lesson time can be used with them to spend time on writing, showing them how to use that specific part of speech to enhance their writing.

◆ More one-on-one time in conferring then leads to changes in their writing. Students better understand the kind of writer that they are, and they can talk about these parts of speech in useful ways.

Our conversations, then, are less about the rote memorization of the parts of speech and more about useful questions. For instance, rather than asking them to define what a pronoun is, I can ask more important questions: "What would happen if we used a pronoun instead of a proper noun here?" or "Why do you think the author chose to use a pronoun here, and does it work? Could the sentence be made better? How?"

As it is done with Constance Weaver's book with Jonathan Bush, *Grammar to Enrich and Enhance Writing:*

the teaching of grammar must be, as we say in Chapter 4, "a mile deep" – meaning that concepts and skills aren't taught just once but are practiced, reviewed, reconsidered in published writing, redeveloped, and made rich through repeated application: the antithesis of "covered."

(2008, p. 201)

Moving from awareness (with the flipped lesson) into practice (during our writing time on Fridays) and then following up with assessment has made the most sense for my students as we go for the "mile deep" kinds of learning, and for me as well.

Now, before I go into discussing what flipped instruction looks like in my classroom, I want to be clear. Though flipped instruction and blended learning has helped my students be more successful, there needs to be follow up activities that accompany the videos that they watch. I don't just set students loose on a video, and hope that it will stick for them when it comes to future use. Furthermore, I don't think flipping on its own is the cure-all to the problems we face as teachers when it comes to grammar. However, I have had some success with flipped learning. For this part of grammar instruction, it has worked for me, and I hope it might work for you as well.

What is Flipping the Classroom, Exactly?

As I am drafting this chapter, it has been almost three years to the day that my principal came to a colleague, our middle school science teacher, and me to discuss the idea of doing flipped instruction to help meet students where they are. In his opinion – and in the opinion of many experts on the entire flipping concept – this means that students are more digital and utilizing the technology they have in front of them for more meaningful purposes. In addition, we were willing to try the flipped approach to see if the turn-in rate was higher for homework. Also, being able to have the lessons at their disposal to review them when needed, we felt it would be beneficial for students who don't retain the information the first time they hear it.

My definition of "flipping" is derived from experts: *Flip Your Classroom: Reach Every Student, in Every Class Every Day* by Jonathan Bergmann and Aaron Sams (2012), and *Flipping 2.0* by Jason Bretzmann (2013). Bergmann and Sams are known for essentially igniting the flipped method of instruction in today's classroom. Bretzmann's text examined many teachers in multiple subjects and how they took the flipped model and integrated into their own classrooms. From what I have learned – and what I have done in my own situation – a flipped classroom is where traditional teaching methods are switched; instruction is delivered through online videos, and links to other online resources such as definitions, exercises, and quizzes. So, the teacher picks the lesson they want to teach, creates a video where the lesson is being taught, and delivers the video to the students so they can watch it outside of the classroom. Ideally, the students come back prepared for an activity that is associated with the lesson.

In other words, the "homework" portion is done in the classroom with the help of the teacher. Homework might include an online assignment, worksheet, project, or partner discussion. With the flipped model, students have more access to teachers to answer questions that they might not otherwise be able to have answered when they are at home. More often these questions can be asked and answered while the student is in class working on the activity associated with the flipped lesson. And, as I noted above, when it comes to writing instruction, I was able to spend more time conferring with students because they viewed the grammar mini-lesson outside of class time. For me, this instruction happened not every day, but on Fridays – a typical day for writing workshop time – after my students had an entire week to complete the flipped lesson.

Critiques of the Flipped Model

Like all trends in education, there are limits to the flipped model. In August of 2012, Katie Ash published an article in *Education Week* responding to the effectiveness of flipped learning and how educators from all levels were evaluating flipped teaching. Andrew Miller, an educational consultant, is quoted in the article: "My concern is that if you're still relying on lecture as your primary mode of getting content across [even with flipped videos], . . . you haven't done anything to shift the type of learning that's occurring" (Ash, 2012). Also, edu-blogger Terry Freedman notes that "Lecturing to students is usually (and rightly, in my view) regarded as an undesirable thing in schools" (Freedman, n.d.).

Ash's article and Freedman's comment both raise a good point about how teachers' lectures are still the predominant form of instruction; one concern with the flipped model is that all we are doing is changing when and where the student hears the lecture. However, we also have to realize that students have a lot going on in their lives and if they have the choice when they can watch the lecture, they may be more likely to watch it. Teacher surveys have actually found that student's attitudes towards instruction have changed in upwards of 80% towards instruction with flipping (Classroom Window & Flipped Learning Network, 2012).

Other critiques of the flipped model are that not all students learn best by simply getting talked at by the teacher through video lessons. Of course, the best teachers realize that students don't learn best by being lectured to, yet sometimes talking to students to give them facts or guidance is clearly necessary. Also, in the best lessons, students do have more than a lecture to watch when it comes to flipped instruction. Often, teachers provide activities associated with the video that students watch. It isn't just a sit-and-get method of teaching; or, in the sense of the Triple E Framework, the lesson is truly being enhanced and extended. Again, it is important that flipped learning not be simply lecturing transferred to video. Teachers should have thoughtful, scaffolded activities whether the lesson is live or flipped.

Over the past few years I have come to realize that flipped instruction is going to be different for everyone and it will look different in individual classrooms no matter what activity or lesson you choose to use it for. A teacher can't simply think that by flipping their instruction, their students are miraculously going to learn more or turn in more of their homework. The challenge is finding what works well for you and especially for your students. What follows are some digital tools that I use to make the flip work in my classroom.

Digital Tools for Flipping Grammar

As I mentioned in Chapter 2, there are some really incredible tools that can be used to help create videos if you are interested in flipping. There are two specific tools that I will highlight in detail. First, I will touch briefly on Touchcast and then later on go into more depth about a tool called Jing. In addition, Troy and I have listed others in Chapter 2 and on the wiki that accompanies the book.

The tools that are available for screencasting range in complexity of use and cost from being free to somewhat expensive. Personally, I prefer a digital tool called Touchcast (www.touchcast.com). That said, Touchcast is what I would put on the "expert" level and I don't want to scare anyone away from trying to do a flipped lesson in their classrooms. Still, I prefer Touchcast because of all the extras that I can incorporate into my videos: green-screen backgrounds, a news ticker across the front of the video, and other similar enhancements.

To keep things simple let's start with some screencasting tools from Techsmith, a software company out of Okemos, Michigan that has three different tools: Jing, Snag-it, and Camtasia. Some simple descriptions of these tools are provided in Chapter 2. In staying aligned with the Triple E Framework, I use these to enhance and extend students' learning, not just as a gimmicky way to catch their attention. For the examples below, I will walk through Jing. Jing is free and, while it does limit both recording time to no more than five minutes, as well as the amount of storage space you are allowed, it is still a great tool to get started with when learning how to screencast.

Now, I will not be spending a whole bunch of time telling you about using the tool; remember, there are many, many tutorials available online, and I invite you to ask your own students to be your guides. Thus, we will be brief on instructions and, instead, we will be talking about how to design scaffolded instructional practices with flipped lessons. I will walk through the process of using my classroom website, the screencasting tool, Jing, and the "Watch, Summarize, Question" (WSQ) tool for students as they view the flipped lessons.

Building a Flipped Video Lesson

First, to give some context for the flipped lessons, I want to mention that I have a website for my students to visit when they need to do their flipped lessons (hyler1.weebly.com). Right now, I use Weebly, which is really great. I love the creative and design aspects that Weebly allows you to make your website appealing. It is also fairly easy for students to navigate through the site. In the past I have used Wikispaces, and I am confident I am going back to using Wikispaces for my classroom website in the 2016–17 school year because I love how the information can be more easily organized in terms of use for teachers and it seems easier for my students to access. No matter what system you use, however if you are going to create flipped lessons, then you should design a space to share them conveniently and in an organized manner.

With a place to house the videos, I can now create them, and this is where you, as a teacher, have choices. Just to be simple, I will start with Jing, a very simple screen capturing tool that allows you to create short screen captures for your students. I will come back to Touchcast later on in the chapter. If you are new to the screen capturing world, Jing is the way to go. It is a very quick and simple download and you get two free gigabytes of memory each month to store your videos. Of course, if you run out of space, you can store them on YouTube, too. Techsmith also has great tutorials for the tool available on their website (please see our wiki for a list of all the links in the book (textingtoteaching.wikispaces.com).

Now, with Jing, you can choose to be recorded with audio alone, or with audio and video. That is not necessarily a problem, but if you want your students to see you, you will need to activate your camera. Jing will only allow you to record a five-minute video. After receiving feedback from my students the first year I implemented flipped lessons, they asked that videos be no longer than five to seven minutes long, so Jing's limited time can actually be a helpful constraint. In most recorded lessons, this is not a problem, but there are times a flipped video might need to be longer. It just depends on the grammar topic. As a self-imposed guideline, I make sure for seventh grade that my videos are no longer than seven minutes and, for eighth graders, they are no longer than eight minutes. Because Jing doesn't allow the user to go over five minutes, more advanced tools such as Snag-it or Touchcast may be used to produce longer videos.

When first creating a flipped lesson, the sound of one's own voice might not be that appealing, and that is completely understandable. I would suggest doing some practice runs before deciding to publish anything. It is totally fine to make mistakes throughout the process. I once recorded a video six times before I was happy with it! Getting comfortable with one's own voice does take some time and, after a few lessons, it may be discovered that the videos should flow a certain way or be organized by a certain format. For me, if I am creating something that I know I will want to use for more than one quick lesson this year, I will write out a brief script with bullet points so I can produce my videos more easily and efficiently knowing they will be saved for posterity. No matter what platform is used for creating, it does take some front-loading in terms of time to create the videos. The payoff, remember, is the time that you, as a teacher, will be able to spend with the students in the classroom during activities such as writing workshop days.

After Jing is downloaded, there is an icon that looks like a yellow sun located at the top-center of the screen (Image 3.1). When hovering over it, three other icons pop down. One is a plus symbol that says "Capture" and this is the one to click on to start recording a flipped lesson. A question that may arise is what to capture? To make things simple, I created my first flipped lesson within a Google Document. I kept it short and simple because I really didn't want to overwhelm myself with a lot of details and I didn't want to overwhelm my students with something that looked complicated and hard to follow. So, I started by creating a video about pronouns. The lesson is on YouTube (https://youtu.be/b0mOw0WCn9Q). I will be going over more

Image 3.1 Jing Controls

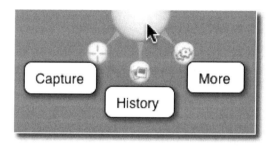

specifics later on in the chapter with this particular lesson. I do have a simple format that I follow for my videos. While I often do not make a formal script or storyboard, you could do that if it is helpful for you. Here is what works for me:

◆ Short greeting
◆ Introduction of grammar concept/skill

  ○ Give a clear definition of concept/skill
  ○ Show examples of concept/skill in isolation and in practice

◆ Read the guided question(s)
◆ Share where they can find addition resources
◆ Remind students of when their "Watch, Summarize, Question" (WSQ) sheets are due
◆ Wish them luck!

Then, I prepare to record. When you click on the plus symbol, a cursor pops up on your screen so you can select what part of your screen you want to capture (Image 3.2). Once you select the area you want to record, a small rectangular box pops up and will ask you whether you want to snap a picture or capture video.

Then when you choose "Capture Video," a message box will pop up and tell you that Jing is ready to record. Then all you need to do is hit the record button and you are on your way to making your first flipped lesson.

When you complete the recording, you simply hit the stop button and Jing will finish what it needs to do with the video before you save it or share it. Before doing so, I would definitely watch it and make sure it is the quality you want to share with your students. Too many times I have finished recording and watched it and realized either my dog is barking or one of my kids might have sneaked into it and I have to re-record. This is the one big disadvantage to Jing and you would have to completely re-record the entire video, which could potentially be very time-consuming.

Image 3.2 Jing Capture Window

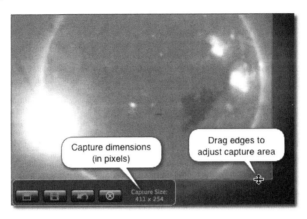

With Jing, you do have the option to save it on your own computer for later access, or you can upload the video to Screencast.com where you get 2 GB of free storage and 2 GB of free bandwidth per month. Screencast will also give you a link that you can provide to your students for viewing. I put a link or an embed code from YouTube onto my website so my students have easy access to the videos. Most of the time I upload videos to YouTube.

Working Through the Video: Steps for Students

It is important to keep in mind how the students are going to watch this video. What do you want your students to do while they are watching it? What kinds of thinking do you want them to engage in?

For me, I want my students to watch the video twice and think about how they can apply the specific grammar skill to their writing. In addition, I want them to know that what they are learning isn't going to be something we do and just forget about it for the rest of the year. I want them to have the mindset that what they are doing is going to have to be applied.

Thus, I create a "guide" for watching the videos. I adapted my guide from Crystal Kirch (2014), and her model that she calls WSQ, pronounced "wisk." Kirch has been a leading teacher in the world of flipping the classroom. She was high school math teacher and is now a digital learning coach where she works with teachers on implementing technology into the classroom in meaningful ways. The WSQ acronym stands for:

- ◆ Watch
- ◆ Summarize
- ◆ Question

Since implementing and adapting Kirch's WSQ model into my classroom, I have changed it to better meet the needs of my students. Again, referring back to the Triple E Framework, I do of course want to engage my students, but I also want to enhance and extend their learning, too. I cover more about WSQ in the specific pronoun lesson and activity outlined in the next section, but you can see the guidelines that my students follow for WSQ in Figure 3.1. The "TMPP" style summary, mentioned on the WSQ handout, will be described later in this chapter. Also, I have a link to this template as well as some completed student examples on the companion wiki for this book.

As the video continues, I then go through and give several examples of personal pronouns for the students to refer to when they are completing their WSQ and for the activities we do in class with it. Keep in mind that while I am doing all of this, the students are not seeing me, they are only hearing me and watching me as I walk them through the use of pronouns. What I hope for is that students will pick up the definition of the grammar skill being taught and be ready to not only define it when they come back to class, but also be able to list examples. Furthermore, by the end of the video I want them to understand how they can apply the skill to their own writing, showing that there is an important purpose for grammar instruction, not just something they have to do to fill time.

Returning to the goals of the Triple E Framework, as I near the end of the flipped lesson, I do two extensions with my students. First, I pose to them what is called a "guided question." This is a question that I want them to go and investigate on their own after the lesson has ended. When I give them the guided questions, I want them to think deeper about the topic and to learn more about it without me being the one doing all the talking. I also give them links where they can go and do the inquiry work. For example, with pronouns, I ask my students: *Why should writers not use too many pronouns in their writing?*

Then, after I pose the question, I would direct them to websites such as Grammar Girl's Quick and Dirty Tips (quickanddirtytips.com) or Grammar Monster (grammar-monster.com). The sites have a search option and are easy to navigate, so students can find the specific grammar topic easily without having to be given too much direction within each site. Both Grammar Girl and Grammar Monster are excellent websites for students to get answers to the guided questions I may ask. I want my students to extend their thinking beyond just knowing the definition of a pronoun. I want them to think about how writers are using these skills and to make conscious moves as writers so they are not just learning the skill and then forgetting it, but applying it to

Figure 3.1 Generic WSQ (Watch, Summarize, Question) Handout

<u>**WSQ for Flipped Lessons**</u>

Topic or Lesson:

-

Summary (Follow TMPP Format):

Example:

-

Guided Question(s) (Copy from Class Website):

-
-

Guided Question(s) Response/Answer:

I can . . .

-

their writing they are working on at the time and their writing in the future. They complete an "I can" statement to wrap up.

Upon completing the video, and if you are pleased with your confident self when you hear the awesomeness in your voice, put that link or embed code on your website and your students are ready to watch their first flipped lesson. Take the time to get a drink and take a deep breath because you probably spent over an hour making your first five minute video, which I am not implying as being negative. But, every once in a while we may want to find other resources that can help us along. GrammarFlip is one source that I trust for doing just that.

Using Flipped Videos from Other Sources

If time is an issue, there is a more recent website that was created for flipped grammar lessons specifically and it is called GrammarFlip (Grammarflip. com), which was created by Anthony Risko. The videos are already made for the teacher in GrammarFlip and it is a free website for both teachers and students where the teacher can set up a class and students can watch the videos that are assigned along with extra practice. I use it with students who need additional practice with the grammar skills that I teach who may not be at grade level.

GrammarFlip is set up differently compared to how I do things in my class. In the videos, you don't see the teacher or the instructor, only Anthony Risko's voice. It is still a lesson about a specific grammar skill and there are still examples for students to see. The site also provides exercises for students to practice. However, I feel that the exercises are leaning more towards the rote, drill and kill approach, which is not what I want for my students. Still, GrammarFlip is a great supplement to my own flipped instruction. I can use it to provide students with the extra support that they need.

Additionally, any search on YouTube will yield dozens, perhaps hundreds, of other lessons from a variety of sources, including the popular Shmoop. Again, these videos can be very helpful and can, at times, be a lifesaver when you just don't have time to create your own flipped lessons. That said, I will share these videos with students only after creating some enhancements using a tool like EdPuzzle, which allows me to build in multiple-choice and short answer questions. The point that I want to make here is this: even if you don't make the flipped lesson, you can still remix and adapt the videos that are out there and add your own personal touch. Building on the ideas of others is what the internet is all about, and sometimes you don't have to do flipping all on your own.

Breaking it Down: Pronouns of the Personal Type

Keeping the Triple E Framework in mind, and layering in the use of Google Docs, let's examine a simple possessive pronouns lesson I do with my seventh graders. As Sean Ruday discusses in his book, *The Common Core Grammar Toolkit*, "[t]he ability to use proper pronoun case is an important skill for writers to possess, as it allows them to clearly express their thoughts and avoid confusing their readers" (p. 15). In addition, Jeff Anderson's *Mechanically Inclined* states that pronouns "stand in for nouns, keeping writing succinct and less repetitive" (p. 104). Remember, a flipped lesson is much more than just putting your lecture on video, so I will walk through what my students do before, during, and after watching a flipped video on pronouns.

Before the Flipped Lesson

When they get started with watching flipped lessons, I like to walk my students through how to do a video first. I start by pulling up a video from the year before or a video from YouTube. As a side note, I really like showing my students the old Schoolhouse Rock clips about parts of speech and grammar. They may sound cheesy, but I always catch students humming or singing the tunes from the videos. Also, my students tell me often that they are upset with me because they get the song stuck in their head! Remember, you can adapt those videos into interactive quizzes with EdPuzzle. At any rate, here are the typical steps I go through with students at the beginning of the year to model the entire process of engaging in a flipped lesson:

- ◆ First, before they even open up their computers, we view a practice video and I do a WSQ sheet together with my students.
- ◆ I then show my students where they can access the videos to the lessons they will learn throughout the year. They are located on my class website where students can watch them on their own. These are videos that are created by me.
- ◆ In addition, I help navigate the students through the two websites I mentioned earlier: Grammar Monster and Grammar Girl. I want to ensure the students can find any information they may need for the guided questions that are part of the WSQ sheet that they have to complete.
- ◆ Finally, when it comes to their WSQ sheets, I give my students a choice of how to hand it in to me:

- ○ Students can access the document from the class website, and they can choose to either print it off and complete it by hand,
- ○ Or, as most of my students do, they can make a copy of the "view only" document in Google Docs and turn it in digitally by sharing their completed form with me.

Typically, after I have all of the logistics out of the way, I assign the flipped lesson at the beginning of the week on Monday. Both my seventh and eighth graders have until Thursday of the same week to complete the flipped lesson. I firmly believe that by giving them multiple days, the process benefits both the student who works at a faster pace and those who work at a slower pace. Furthermore, students have sports and other extracurricular activities that are, let's face it, more important to them than a grammar lesson. So, the extra days do help with the percentage of homework completion, but it is not a fix-all to the missing homework epidemic that plagues us all. In a typical week, my students spend two to three days in a writing workshop setting. There are many factors that play into the number of days they spend writing, however, so it does vary.

During the Flipped Lesson

Now that the students have been walked through what they need to do, they have a few days to complete the task of watching their lesson. While the students are watching the video, I ask them to do some things that assure me that they have both watched the video and are prepared for the activity that we will do on Friday during workshop time. As mentioned earlier in the chapter, the "W" stands for Watch, as in "watch" the video, but I ask my students to watch the video twice. The first time I want them to just concentrate on the video and not worry about filling out the WSQ form. My hope is that they focus more on what the video is trying to teach them, instead of them worrying about filling in the WSQ sheet. Now, whether they actually take the time to watch the video twice is something I can't necessarily check. Students don't tell me whether they do or don't watch it twice, but, with the guided questions, it is difficult for students to gain all the information that they need without watching it twice.

The students have now watched the video and it is time to fill in the "S," which stands for summarize. As a middle school staff, we have adopted a common way for our students to summarize. We call the process TMPP and it is outlined in Figure 3.2. The process was adapted from the acronym TDPP from the book *Get It Done!: Writing and Analyzing Informational Texts*

Figure 3.2 Summary Paragraph (TMPP Format)

<u>Summary Paragraph (TMPP Format)</u>

- **Introduce the (T)opic**
- **Describe the (M)ain ideas that support the topic**
- **Explain what (P)oint is being made about the topic (Why is this important?)**
- **Write a wra(P)-up sentence to bring your summary to a close**

to Make Things Happen (Exceeding the Common Core State Standards) by Jeff Wilhelm, Michael Smith, and Jim Fredricksen (2012, p. 87). As a middle school staff, we want our students to know how to summarize well. So, without all the subject areas getting something different each time students are asked to summarize, we decided that we wanted a common approach. The TMPP process (Figure 3.2) is one that is taught to seventh graders at the very beginning of the year so they can effectively write summaries wherever they are needed. Students have already practiced this extensively before the flipped lessons and the WSQ sheet have been introduced, so it is my hope that students can share a nicely written summary about the grammar skill that is being taught on the video.

Notice the TMPP summary is for a single paragraph. We do adapt it for summaries that may need to be longer, but I don't require my students to write any more that a paragraph when it comes to the flipped lesson. My focus isn't on whether or not they can write a long summary, but that they are clearly understanding what it is that they learned from the video. Below is a student example of a summary written for personal pronouns. Colton, an eighth grader wrote:

> Personal Pronouns represent people or things. The Personal Pronouns are I, you, he, she, it, we, and they. Sometimes when we use Pronouns too much it can mislead people. We use personal Pronouns so we don't have to keep repeating a same person's name. When using a Personal Pronoun you don't want to start with one if the reader doesn't know who you are talking about. Only start a sentence with a Personal Pronoun if the reader knows who you are talking about. Other Pronouns include Subjective and Objective Pronouns.

In this summary, Colton has shown that he has a clear understanding of pronouns. He has comprehended that if he uses pronouns too much in his writing, he will confuse his readers. Colton also understands that he has to be cautious with the moves he makes as a writer before he actually uses pronouns. He understands that a proper noun should be used first, followed by a pronoun. After reading Colton's summary, I am confident he will be able to effectively use pronouns in his writing.

When students complete the summary portion of their WSQ outline, I then ask them to provide me with an example of the skill being taught. In this instance, I ask students to list some personal pronouns and I require them to give me an example in a sentence. Sadly, if I do not clarify what they need to put in the example section, I feel that they will do as little as possible when filling it out. Maybe that is just the nature of middle school students! Thus, I always try to give them a specific directive when it comes to this section of the WSQ sheet.

By providing me with an example so that I can see them using the learned skill, the students then move on to complete the Q part of WSQ. This particular part is by far my favorite because students get to inquire about the skill they are learning and they come up with some great questions that lead to some outstanding discussions in class. For example, with pronouns I had middle school students ask:

◆ *Can every proper noun be made into a pronoun?* – Casey
◆ *What are the differences between personal pronouns and possessive personal pronouns?* – Naomi
◆ *Is "my" a possessive pronoun?* – Kamrey

I could provide a plethora of examples of the questions students ask, so it shows me that they are, indeed, thinking deeply. More important to note here is what the flipped lesson – in contrast to a typical grammar worksheet – enables students to do. By giving the students opportunities to ask questions, they become part of the learning process and they are taking charge of their learning. Again, harkening back to the Triple E, the use of the flipped lesson format, including the video and the WSQ sheet, allows students to enhance and extend their learning, not just engage with technology.

The questions the students provide form the basis of what we review in class. Don't get me wrong, I don't address every question that students have. Sometimes students either ask questions that aren't all that inquisitive, or I might just answer them as a comment on the WSQ sheet when I provide feedback. It is essential that you model what type of questions you are looking for with your students or you might get some ridiculous ones. Students should not be asking me whether or not I am going to the game on Friday night! I definitely mark them down for questions that are irrelevant to the topic.

Moving along in the same realm of questioning, the students then answer the guided question(s) that are posed with the video or, perhaps, even in the video. Guided question(s) are those questions that I give to the students so they can think further about the lesson. This past year, when it came to pronouns, I asked the students two guided questions. For instance, with pronouns:

1. Why shouldn't we use too many pronouns in our writing?
2. What other types of pronouns can you think of when it comes to your writing besides personal pronouns? How would you use those pronouns?

Answers varied for both guided questions, and that's just fine with me. To be clear, the overall goal is for the students to think more critically about pronouns and not just hurry up and get the assignment done. Furthermore, I want students to adequately apply the grammar skills they are learning to their writing.

As students are wrapping up the WSQ sheet, there is one last section that I have on the form. I want my students to fill in an "I can . . ." statement. These types of statement are usually geared more towards elementary-aged students, but I want my students to understand what they are trying to achieve with learning each grammar lesson. Some "I can . . ." statements that I have received from my students include:

◆ *I can write a sentence that includes one or more personal pronouns* – Aubrey
◆ *I can become a better writer by changing nouns to pronouns when necessary* – Elliot

I feel it is important for them to know what the goals are for them when it comes to the curriculum. In addition, I believe my students have a better understanding that there is a purpose for what I assign to them. We are not just "doing grammar" to take up time or meet a random standard. They understand that they are trying to become better writers.

When they are done, I encourage them to double check it and hand it in to me. Some students get it done earlier, some wait until the last minute. Figure 3.3 gives you an idea of what a completed WSQ outline looks like when the student finishes. The example that is provided is one that I would expect every student to turn in. In other words, it has been done well. Remember, just as a reminder, students have from Monday until Thursday to watch the video and complete the WSQ.

Figure 3.3 Sample of Completed Student WSQ Assignment

WSQ

Topic or Lesson: Pronouns

Summary (Follow TMPP): Personal Pronouns are used to represent a person or a thing. The personal pronouns are "they," "I," "you," "he," "she," "it," and "we." Pronouns can be used to make your writing more focused and less confusing. Pronouns help without having to repeat a person's name. Pronouns, are words that can be used to substitute proper nouns. They are important to help make us better writers.

Example: I was wondering about Tyler. Did he go to the football game with you last night?

Question: Can you use the same pronoun twice in one sentence?

Guided Question(s) (Answers)

1. What happens if we use too many pronouns?
    a. If we use too many pronouns in our writing the reader may not be able to follow along very well and get confused.
2. What other types of pronouns are there?
    a. When I searched the sites, I found something called a relative pronoun. They connect clauses and phrases and there are a lot of relative pronouns that start with the letter W.

I can . . . use a pronoun to represent something or someone's name in a sentence.

After the Flipped Lesson

Now comes the part of the lesson that I truly enjoy. Also, I know that my students look forward to Friday when we are working with our flipped grammar lessons during writing workshop time. This is where I try to help the students incorporate the lesson that they learned into their writing so it is not being taught in isolation.

I mentioned before that I collect the WSQ sheets on Thursday. I grade them and hand them back to the students who turned in hard copies; students who turned them in digitally grab their laptop so they can see the grade they received. Then, we take time as a class to go over the questions students wrote down on their WSQ sheets. So, if they ask a question similar to the one in Figure 3.3, we would go over examples on the board. I would have them get out *The Outsiders* by S. E. Hinton (1967), the novel we are reading while doing pronouns, and see if the author was doing what the student asked. If students find examples, I will have them use our document camera to show where they found the example. I typically give 10–15 minutes for discussing questions. This allows time for the students who did not finish their assignment of watching the flipped lesson to go into the hallway and do the lesson while the rest of us are engaging in a conversation about pronouns or the other grammar topics that are at hand. Now, I know there are teachers who might say students are still missing the lesson. The motivation for students to complete their lesson is engaging in the activity. The idea of flipping is to take less class time explaining the concept and more on applying what the student learns. By having students going in the hall and completing a three to four minute video, they can finish quickly and jump into the planned activity without missing a beat. This provides students who aren't typically engaged to become more interested in what is happening surrounding grammar.

After we have discussed the questions and those who have not watched the video are done, I now direct every student to get out their laptop and access their grammar folder that they have made in Google Documents at the beginning of the year. We then start building their personal grammar guide (discussed in more detail in the next section) which can take 20–25 minutes. This then gives my students about 30 minutes to work on their current writing assignment.

Now, to be clear, my students are not just assessed on grammar through their WSQ sheets alone. I have my students apply what they have learned into their current writing assignment, which, in this case, is their personal memoir. I have my students highlight where they are using pronouns so I can see they have accurately applied what they have learned to their writing. By building their grammar folder throughout the year, it helps them to have a reference point for when they work on their writing.

Building a Personal Grammar Guide

One of the things that I have felt that my students didn't do well enough in the past was seeking out resources when they had questions about parts of speech or other items related to grammar. So, one of the first things I have my students create is a grammar resources folder in their Google Drive at the beginning of the year. Within that folder they create separate documents for each grammar lesson they have throughout the school year. This practice is adapted from what Jeff Anderson did with his students with their writer's notebook, as he describes in *Mechanically Inclined*. Just like Anderson, I want my students to retain these grammatical concepts. He argues that "[g]iving students scaffolds in the forms of examples and visual inserts for their writer's notebooks to help them start and continue collecting" (p. 12) is critical, and I agree.

To begin, I have the students do three things in their documents:

1. Create a table that includes the definition of the skill along with several examples.

   a. For example, in Figure 3.4, an eighth grade student has written the definition of a personal pronoun and listed both personal and possessive personal pronouns in her table.

2. Next, students show examples of pronouns being used in mentor texts.

   a. With pronouns, my eighth graders were reading *The Outsiders* by S. E. Hinton, so we were using that as our mentor text at the time.

3. Finally, I have students write out at least two sentences on their own that show they can identify a pronoun in their own writing. Figure 3.4 shows a completed grammar page in a student's grammar folder they have created in Google Documents.

This is not the only time they are doing activities or anything with pronouns. As we read through *The Outsiders*, the students are also doing a personal memoir. One of the requirements that I have for them when they are doing their memoir is to include and identify five personal pronouns and five possessive personal pronouns. Whenever my students are applying the skill they have learned to their own writing I have them highlight it in a specific color. For example, with pronouns I would have my students highlight their use of pronouns in blue using the highlight feature in Google Docs. Furthermore, I always do a follow-up reflection writing with my students and ask them questions about the moves they make as writers. Within those questions, I do ask them about why they used certain parts of speech in the places they did in their writing. I want my students to be consciously thinking about the way they write.

Figure 3.4 Sample of Student Personal Pronoun Usage Guide

Personal Pronouns

Personal Pronoun:	A pronoun that is used to refer to a speaker or someone that the speaker is referring to in writing.
Personal Pronoun examples:	I, we, they, he, she, you
Possessive Personal Pronoun examples:	Mine, yours, theirs his, hers, ours

The Outsiders **by S. E. Hinton**	"Then *I* saw Johnny." "*He* was sitting next to *me*, one elbow on *his* knee, and staring straight ahead.*"*

Personal Pronoun Sentence	*He* went to the store to so *she* could have milk.
Possessive Personal Pronoun Sentence	It was *their* beach, so *his* ball had to stay there.

Yes, the above example is simple. It isn't some new flashy piece of technology that is going to wow your students. In fact, it could be done just in a writer's notebook. However, I want my students to have access to their grammar guides for quick reference anywhere they go, whether that be another class, at home, or when they are on vacation completing their homework. In addition, I feel that by students actually writing out examples and seeing how other writers use the grammar skills they are learning, it will then stick with them better. So far, it is working better than just giving them worksheets to test their knowledge. As you can see in Nate's memoir piece (Image 3.3), he can use and identify proper nouns in his writing. Furthermore, students can think about the moves they make as writers, which you will see more of in Chapter 4. Next, we will look at more specific lessons and activities with adverbs, adjectives, and pronouns.

Image 3.3 Nate's Memoir

Rabbit Hunting

Its was a sunny and snowy day and Pat, my dad I were walking out to the woods. We were dressed in warm winter cloths and had our hunters orange on. I asked to go rabbit hunting that morning. My dad said we could. We ate breakfast and waited a while. We got our hunting clothes out of the closets. I put on my snow pants, boots, gloves, a hot and a sweatshirt. I waited for my dad to finish putting on his snow gear. My

Adverbs and Adjectives

We know that pronouns are only one element of the parts of the speech picture. There are many other parts of speech we could explore and play with first, but the use of adverbs and adjectives will help with scaffolding to Chapter 4, where we will discuss the types of sentences and the different writing spaces where students can write, both formally and informally. How does the meaning of the sentence change with regard to adverbs and adjectives? Also, why did the author choose to use the adverbs and adjectives that they did in their story? These are the questions that I ask my students as I have them explore the world of adverbs and adjectives. Like Gretchen Bernabei discusses in her book *Grammar Keepers* (p. 214), I, too, want students to think about the intentional moves they make as well as why they make the choices they make as writers.

As with pronouns, prior to doing any activities related to adverbs and adjectives, my middle school students have already watched their flipped lesson (available on our wiki). I typically do this grammar lesson when my seventh graders are studying, and will eventually write their own, myths. I want my seventh graders to be creative when it comes to their writing. As they enter middle school, I want them to stop using "dead words" such as "sad," "mad," "happy," and "said." Furthermore, I want them to realize that there is more to using adjectives than just using "color words." In terms of my eighth graders, they are reading *Behind Rebel Lines* by Seymour Reit and have just finished their Civil War unit in social studies, where they will be writing a Civil War research paper. The student examples I show you from this activity will be from my students' work in that unit, even though it could really be adapted using any mentor text.

Because students are accustomed to using text messaging, I use the website "iOS 7 Text" (ios7text.com), which is free, and allows them to compose fake text messages. The website does not require a username or password, though students can even put their name on the "phone" shown on screen. The one downfall that my students and I have discovered with this tool is that it is rather difficult to delete texts that are written in the text bubbles. More often than not, my students have had to refresh the page to start over when they have made mistakes. Still, it meets the first level of "Engagement" in the Triple E Framework, and it helps us move beyond it, too.

Using or mirroring text messaging while learning adverbs and adjectives can effectively teach students to be more descriptive in their writing. Oftentimes I am reiterating to my students that they need to be more descriptive in their writing, no matter what spaces they may write in. My thinking is this: if students can write descriptively in their social spaces, they can use this to scaffold to their more formal writing assignments. When students are done, they do need to use a screen capturing tool so they can send me a copy of what they have completed. My students just use the simple Snip-it tool that is already on the PC computers. It is a tool that students have been introduced to in their technology class. Now, the website gives you an option to like their page on Facebook, but because Facebook is blocked at our school and I don't necessarily want my students accessing social media at school, I just have them send me a screen capture via email.

Now that some of the logistics are out of the way, I first review with the students adverbs and adjectives. I feel that teaching adverbs and adjectives together works well. I tell my students that adverbs are adjectives for verbs and that they tell us when, where, how often, and how much. The students at this point have made a grammar page in their Google Docs that I ask them to access at the beginning of the activity. After reviewing with them I then proceed to give them a mentor sentence from *Behind Rebel Lines* that contains adjectives and adverbs. I start with: "The huge supply tent, pitched near the courthouse, was chaotic, but somehow everything worked efficiently" (p. 7). The students easily identify "huge" and "chaotic" as adjectives and the word "efficiently" as an adverb. From here, I have them do a pair-share and have them discuss why they think the author used these particular words in the sentence. I then open it up to a class discussion, and I simulate some of the typical responses that students offer in the fictional exchange below:

Mia:	I think the word "huge" was used to show how big the tent was.
Mr. Hyler:	What would happen if I changed that adjective to something completely different or I substituted a different synonym?
Clayton:	If I used the word "fluffy" instead of "huge," it isn't about the size of the tent anymore.
Mr. Hyler:	Good point, Clayton, it is now about the material of the tent instead of how big the tent is.
Dakota:	If you use a synonym or even an antonym, it doesn't really have the same effect unless you were to use "gigantic" or something like that.
Mr. Hyler:	Right, Dakota, and if the author used the word "tiny," we would know that the tent wasn't very big. Now, what about the adverb used?

The conversation continues and we move forward with class and small group discussions about the sentence. Then, I introduce the students to the fake texting website that I mentioned above and let the students play around with it for five to ten minutes. I do show them the basics, but for the most part, I just let them play around to get a sense of how it works before describing the activity in detail.

Once the students have had some time to tinker, I put their list of expectations for the activity on the projector or whiteboard. The bulleted list shows how I set it up for the student in terms of who their audience is when they are writing.

- ◆ As a student of text messaging, you, the writer, are responsible for sending a text to one of your friends (your audience) whom you would normally communicate with using your phone.
    - ○ Using the fake text site, copy the mentor sentence from *Behind Rebel Lines* in a new text box.
    - ○ Next, change the two adjectives and one adverb in the sentence either using synonyms or antonyms in another text box. The meaning of the sentence can change.
    - ○ Explain why the author might have made the moves that he did and also explain why you changed what you did.
    - ○ NOTE: Digitalk is allowed, but not in the mentor sentence. Think about how you normally address your friend(s) when you send them text messages.
- ◆ Use the Snip-it tool or take a screenshot and send it to Mr. Hyler's email. Put "Adverbs & Adjectives" in the subject line.
- ◆ The purpose of this activity is to show how you can write in an informal writing space while still using adverbs and adjectives effectively.

I give my students 20–30 minutes to work on the activity. After I finish grading it, I show what was turned in via my projector. I don't go through every student's writing, but I draw on some random students. In Image 3.4 both students did a great job, but only George shows how he can go back and forth between formal and informal writing (Chapter 4) with his "digitalk." Alli's shows what the sentence might look like if an antonym was used instead of a synonym.

As mentioned previously, the eighth graders work on a Civil War research paper where they get to pick their topic and form a thesis. This is an outstanding paper for them to work on adverbs and adjectives because it offers them an opportunity to be descriptive about a moment in our nation's history that should, indeed, be described appropriately and with detail.

For both seventh and eighth grade, I really want them to show me that they have command over these two different parts of speech and to get rid

Image 3.4 Text Messages

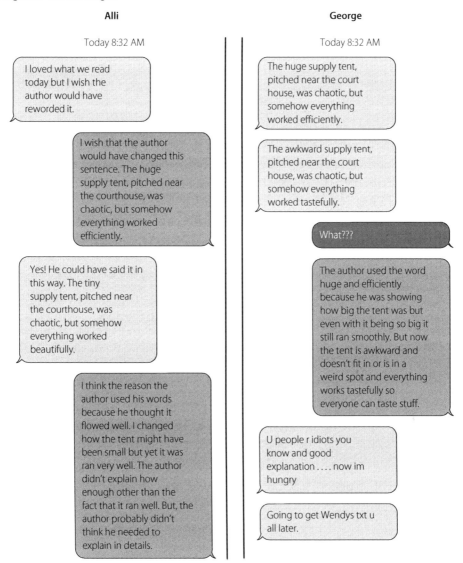

of the constant dead words that tend to pop up in their paper. For both the myths my seventh graders compose, and the research paper my eighth graders write, I have them highlight their use throughout their papers. Typically, I have seventh graders highlight ten adjectives and eighth graders have to highlight fifteen. Adverbs and adjectives are great parts of speech to revisit with this same activity several times throughout the year. The students do not get bored with it and it is a great scaffolding exercise for when they use the social media templates for types of sentences.

Next Steps

There are many parts of speech that we could have discussed in the book, but then we would have a book about parts of speech, not about demonstrating how my students are becoming more engaged with different grammar exercises using flipped lessons to engage and extend their use of pronouns as well as the iOS text tool to enhance and extend their understanding of adjectives and adverbs. Each of the above activities could be adapted to nouns or verbs, conjunctions or interjections, articles or prepositions.

While keeping parts of speech themselves at the core of these types of lessons, it is also necessary to think strategically about the use of the technology. For my students, I want the bridge being created between their real lives and what they learn as mentioned in the "Extend" level of the Triple E Framework. Questions like "Does the technology create a bridge between school learning and everyday life experiences?" and "Does the technology allow students to build skills that they can use in their everyday lives?" help guide me to implementing technology in meaningful ways.

As we think about parts of speech, we can then begin to reimagine sentences as a whole, and how changing the parts of speech can also change the sentence itself. Types of sentences and sentence structure depend on those parts of speech we examined in this chapter. Chapter 4 discusses how formal and informal writing is crucial for student success. In addition, we will look at sentence combining using a tool called Lino, using Twitter to write compound sentences, and also using Google Slides to compose the variety of sentences that exist to help students better understand those types of sentences – and the moves authors make as writers – so they may mirror those moves in their own writing.

4

Learning Sentence Style with Formal and Informal Writing

Parts of speech are only a fraction of the grammar picture. I try not to spend too much time focusing on parts of speech because it should be a review for most students. Thinking back to the conversation that I had with the students mentioned at the beginning of Chapter 3, however, there are items that do have to be revisited from time to time!

As any language arts teacher knows, once the students have the basics down with the different parts of speech, then they can start creating and crafting some miraculous sentences. I explain to my students that sentences can be similar to putting together a puzzle where you are fitting words, phrases, and clauses together. The difference with sentences is that there is more than one way to put the puzzle together and it can always be changed.

Playing with formal and informal sentences gives students the chance to explore several spaces in which they could potentially see and use different types of sentences and explore where formal and informal writing is indeed appropriate. The ways in which we use various technologies to compose is both a function of the technology itself and the social context in which it is used. For instance, Twitter, by its limited number of characters (which looks like it may be changing at the time we were writing this book, but is currently 140), forces us to be clear and concise. In my classroom, I ask for student input on the spaces they converse in the most. Towards the beginning of the year, the following spaces get the most hits for student interaction:

- ◆ Twitter
- ◆ Facebook
- ◆ E-mail
- ◆ Google Document or Word Document
- ◆ Text Messaging
- ◆ Instagram, Snapchat, or other photo sharing services

While I try to help my students become better writers, especially with sentence types and what spaces they are writing these sentences, I don't want to take away their own use of language when they are writing in the different spaces they visit the most. As mentioned earlier, Kristen Hawley Turner, a professor at Fordham University has written articles on code switching and the way students use what she labels as "digitalk." Turner writes, "I see digitalk as a complex and fascinating combination of written and conversational languages that adolescents use when they text, when they instant message (IM), and when they participate in social networks" (Turner, 2009, p. 37). Students today have found their own language and ways to communicate with their peers that is easy for them to understand in an informal way. This is not new; slang is something that has been studied intently by linguists for over 50 years, and has been going on for even longer. Some educators feel strongly that technology is to blame for students' lack of language and grammar skills today. However, we can't chastise students for using the letter "u" to represent the word "you" or how they spell "love," "luv." It is their language. For me, I see it as an opportunity to teach my students the difference between formal and informal writing. I want my students to know I respect their own language, but want to show them when it is appropriate for them to use it. They need to know when and where code switching is necessary.

Code Switching

The phrase sounds like some sort of top secret government operative, but code switching is not a new term, or even a new way of doing things in the classroom. Realistically, we do it every day and so do our students. Simply put, code switching is an individual's choice of a dialect or language over another, depending on different cultural or social situations in which a person has an identity. Think of how a parent might speak or write differently to their child in comparison to how they might talk to another adult.

Code switching has been a distinct topic of conversation that goes back as far as the 1960s when schools were de-segregated and different language dialects were being spoken within the classroom. More recently, Turner has also written an article in *English Journal* about the idea of students using their own language and teaching our students to code switch. "Using text speak as an example of code-switching may acknowledge the legitimacy of the language while bringing its use to the conscious level, where students can choose to use it or not, depending on the context" (Turner, p. 61). Turner's comment hits home hard for me with the activities I am doing with my students on a weekly, and sometimes daily, basis.

Digging even deeper into code switching, according to the article *"Codeswitching: Tools of Language and Culture Transform the Dialectally Diverse Classroom"* by Rebecca S. Wheeler and Rachel Swords, there is the common misconception that only one "'standard'" (2004, p. 474) exists for teaching English to students, when in fact there are formal and informal standards that do exist and can be easily taught to students. Furthermore, students can truly identify the differences between formal and informal English standards when given the opportunity to practice code switching. Bottom line, I want my students to be able to know when to use "digitalk" and when not to use it when it comes to their own writing. Thus, we explore the process of composing sentences using a variety of digital tools, engaging students as well as enhancing and extending their learning along the way.

Compound, Complex, and Complete: Making Sentences Matter

While keeping code switching and the times students should write formally or informally in mind, the rest of the chapter is set up to show how I scaffold students through a series of lessons using tools such as Lino, Twitter, and Google Slides. The Google Slides activity that is discussed last appears to be quite elaborate, but, in reality, takes no time at all once students have gone through it a few times.

As I've described throughout the book so far, I have shifted the way I teach grammar to my middle school students. In Chapter 2 of *Mechanically Inclined*, Jeff Anderson states, "To develop fluency in grammar and mechanics, students need quick daily instruction and practice" (p. 19). So, I knew that I had to come up with some quick activities that could be used almost daily and not take a ton of time because of the other curricula I needed to teach. With the types of sentences – compound, complex, and compound-complex – I use technologies not only to teach the students about the effective use of sentences, but also to help them create multiple resources so they can refer to rules or examples when implementing certain types of sentences into their own writing.

Furthermore, I want my students to be able to identify the different audiences they are writing for on a daily basis and practice the skills they have learned when possible. That way my students can practice their code switching when they are writing in formal and informal spaces. Thus, teaching them the different sentence varieties and practicing the use of sentences in their everyday writing is crucial for their continued success.

As students learn to vary their sentences, they become more flexible as writers – a skill which is more important now than ever. Remember, "flexibility is now perhaps the most prized goal of writing instruction because the fully proficient writer can adapt to different contexts, formats, and purposes for writing" (Graham & Perin, p. 22). Today, students have to learn to write in different spaces and for real-life purposes. Teachers should understand the different contexts (school, work, and personal) where students write, and help them explore the differences in those contexts. Our goal as educators should be to create proficient writers that can "adapt their writing to its context . . . [and] move among purposes that range from writing solely for themselves (as in a personal diary) to communicating with an external audience" (Graham & Perin, p. 22).

How can we help students become more flexible? As Graham and Perin argue in *Writing Next: Effective Strategies to Improve Writing of Adolescents in Middle and High Schools*, one key strategy is sentence combining. They define it this way:

> Sentence-combining is an alternative approach to more traditional grammar instruction. Sentence-combining instruction involves teaching students to construct more complex and sophisticated sentences through exercises in which two or more basic sentences are combined into a single sentence.

(p. 18)

When the *Writing Next* study was conducted, it was shown that sentence combining had a moderate effect in improving students' writing. So, I wanted my students to be able to "flex" their grammar muscles by adapting some of the strategies I've learned from Jeff Anderson and take into consideration what Graham and Perin are asking educators to do with sentence combining. Then, we would layer in digital tools as well. Through the use of Google Slides for different writing spaces, Twitter for crafting short and powerful sentences, and using a site called Lino for sentence combining, my students are using digital tools to help them become more fluent writers beginning with sentences.

In Chapter 3, I discussed how I have adapted the use of a writer's notebook from what Jeff Anderson has done with his students to create their own ongoing grammar guides in Google Docs. I particularly love how Anderson constantly uses mentor texts with his students to analyze sentences. He focuses on punctuation, grammar, and sentence structure. While helping the students understand sentences, Anderson requires his students to use a writer's notebook throughout the year and he has them use "sentence strips" around the room. So, in other words, if the students are working on compound sentences, they write out examples of compound sentences on long sheets of paper (the aforementioned sentence strips), and post them in a designated spot where they can be referred to when students need examples to use in their own writing.

Anderson's students are allowed to play freely in the notebooks he provides. He wants them to be a space where students understand they are a valued member of his class. Furthermore, students can feel comfortable enough to make mistakes while developing their writing skills. Anderson's students also outline specific sections where they might focus on skills such as sentence patterns, paragraphs that work well for authors, or even simple phrases that his students find throughout mentor texts. As a teacher who implements various digital tools into the classroom, this is where I take what Anderson does further by thinking about the different spaces that they are writing in. My goal is to help them understand and use a few grammatical concepts related to sentences. Specifically, they need to know the following:

◆ Coordinating conjunctions – A word used to connect to independent clauses.
◆ Subordinating conjunctions – A word used to join a subordinating clause (dependent clause) to an independent clause.
◆ Dependent clauses – A clause that cannot stand alone as a sentence.
◆ Independent clauses – A clause that can stand alone as a sentence.

Working with the different types of sentences, I have developed lessons and activities that best meet the needs of my students with the implementation of technology where I feel I am reaching more students on a daily basis. So, let's examine sentence combining and revision with a variety of technology tools, all the while working to enhance and extend students' abilities as writers.

Sentence Combining with Lino

Reflecting on what I used to do in my classroom a few years ago, I think it is amazing my students learned anything at all from me! Okay, seriously, I do think they learned something, but it's no wonder they dreaded coming to English class. Worksheets, grammar handbooks, and repeated examples on the whiteboard or overhead projector were all slowly putting my students into sleep mode.

Now, when it comes to sentence combining, I will admit, I was not having my students engaged in the process that much prior to implementing technology into my lessons. I really don't have an answer as to why; I had learned about the sentence combining method, I just wasn't doing it. On occasion, I might have students put sentences (or the words in the sentences) on note cards or pieces of cardstock and have them physically move the pieces around, but I never had them take chunks of a sentence and move them around. I was more interested in students just knowing the different types of sentences (declarative, interrogative, imperative, and exclamatory) and that they should be putting a capital letter at the beginning as well as a punctuation mark at the end.

When I was starting to work on this book with Troy and was reintroduced to the idea of sentence combining, it clicked with me that students would be able to not only comprehend more of what makes up a particular type of sentence, but that they could actually be able to play with the parts of sentences. By shifting and moving the different parts, their "playing" with sentences would help when they are creating sentences in their own writing.

Similar to Jeff Anderson, I want my students to play with mentor texts from the novels or the readings we do in class. With this particular lesson, I want my students to work on taking a sentence apart and combining it together in different ways. One of the big questions I ask my students during this activity is, "Could the author have said the same thing with a different sentence?" At the end of them playing with the sentence, I then ask them about the type of sentence that they have created. I like to introduce this activity to my seventh graders when they are reading *Roll of Thunder, Hear My Cry* by Mildred Taylor (1976).

My students use an online tool called Lino (en.linoit.com). Lino is an online sticky note site. It is completely free and even offers potential users the opportunity to see all its features before signing up for an account. Yes, that's right, this is a free tool, too. In terms of the Triple E Framework, I feel this tool helps to scaffold the students into other lessons and activities that we do later on in the year and with other grammar concepts as well. This past year, I didn't have my students sign up for an account because I was curious how Lino worked and I know there are other sticky note platforms available for teachers. A tool such as Padlet (padlet.com) could be used for the same type of lesson I am describing here.

I always like to give my students time to play. So after introducing them to Lino, I give them 10 minutes to familiarize themselves with the tool. Then, I introduce them to the assignment. We begin by looking at the sentence on page 102 of *Roll of Thunder, Hear My Cry,* which is a novel my seventh graders read just after Christmas.

> The blue-black shine that had so nicely encircled T. J.'s left eye for over a week had almost completely faded by the morning T. J. hopped into the back of the wagon beside Stacey and snuggled in a corner not occupied by the butter, milk, and eggs Big Ma was taking to sell at the market in Strawberry.
>
> (Taylor, p. 102)

I ask my students what type of sentence they think is written here: compound, complex, compound-complex, or perhaps just a run-on. I get every sentence type answer. It is a difficult sentence for seventh graders to assess. Many of my students get hung up here and have to re-read the sentence more than once. Though I struggle with this sentence myself, my students and I come to the conclusion that this sentence could potentially be a run-on or just a really long simple sentence. My students do wonder if the author wrote the sentence as it is on purpose. They feel that the sentence could be re-written to be less confusing and they do question the effectiveness of the sentence as it is written. However, to be clear and to keep code switching in mind, the author was probably trying to capture dialect in this instance for effect. Thus, I am very excited to discuss this sentence and I feel it is a great sentence for them to take apart and play with using Lino. So, I have my students:

1. Copy the mentor sentence from *Roll of Thunder, Hear My Cry* from page 102 using a sticky note from Lino.
2. Using a different color sticky note, break the mentor sentence into several pieces. (I don't require them to have a certain number, I want them to be free to break it up how they see fit. Image 4.1 shows how one student broke it up into five parts.)
3. Rearrange the sentence to make a new type of sentence or sentences.
4. Create a new sticky note in a third color that describes the moves they made as an author, and why you made those moves as a writer.
5. Take a screenshot of your screen using your Snip-it tool and share with Mr. Hyler via email. Put Lino in the subject line.

It takes approximately 50–60 minutes to do the activity with my seventh graders. By the time we do an example together, they have time to play

Image 4.1 Screenshot of a student revising a mentor sentence with Lino

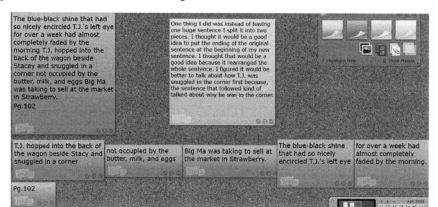

with the tool, and I give them their guidelines, the students have about 15–20 minutes to complete the activity.

Lino allows my students to move and play with parts of sentences in an online space other than where they normally spend time doing their writing assignments (Google Documents). By clicking and dragging the different sticky notes around, they are treating the sentence like a puzzle and trying to see what can work and what can't work for the audience they are writing for. It saves time, too, when students don't have to rewrite parts on notecards and then lose them. Furthermore, I am not taking any papers home with me to grade; the links that students send are in a folder that I have created in my email inbox.

Though it may be hard to see exactly how my students are taking this activity with them to their own writing without literally seeing my students in the process of a writing workshop, my seventh grade students did a sentence revision station during our writing workshop time. The revisions that students make use what they did with the *Roll of Thunder, Hear My Cry* sentence activity. The station was specifically designed for students to take two to three of their sentences and not only rewrite them, but rearrange the sentences within their argument papers to improve their sentences (Figure 4.1). The students were encouraged to use Lino for this and then transfer their new sentence to Google Documents. Then, during the reflection process, they were asked to discuss those moves they made as writers.

Figure 4.1 Sample revisions after Lino activity

Original Sentence	Student's Revised Sentence
As you can see, ice cream is better than slushies because it is healthier.	Because ice cream appears to be healthier than slushies, it is the better choice to eat.

The seventh grade student, Sarah, took her original sentence, which was a wrap-up sentence at the end of a paragraph, and changed it from a compound sentence with a transition at the beginning to a complex sentence using the subordinating conjunction "because." Sarah stated that her reason for changing this sentence was that she was trying to eliminate the overuse of the transition "as you can see." In addition, she wrote in her reflection that she wanted to get better at writing complex sentences to improve the sentence variety in her own writing. Because Sarah and other students are actively applying the activity they have done with Lino, for me, the activity is worth doing again with my students, especially when they can see the moves that writers are making using different mentor texts.

Like Jeff Anderson, we use the activity to think carefully about writing. Anderson and his students are constantly looking at mentor texts and analyzing the moves that authors make with different types of sentence structure. Anderson then has his students use their writer's notebook to break down the sentences where students have the opportunity to "play" with the sentences, rearranging them with different beginnings, conjunctions, or other grammatical forms. Furthermore, he has the students create tables in their journals where they write down different nouns, adjectives, and adverbs that were used throughout the mentor text. In addition, he allows his students to discuss what works well for the author with the particular sentences. How we accomplish similar goals using Twitter is what I describe next.

I Tawt I Taw a Tweet Sentence

Who can resist Tweety Bird? I know I couldn't when I watched cartoons, though my students don't always appreciate my impersonation when I introduce this lesson based on Twitter.

Needless to say, I love doing sentence strips with my students, but I enjoy it even more when my students take the idea to Twitter and share their writing with the world because, believe it or not, I feel that students have remarkable things to say and remarkable ways of saying them. To help my students understand the definition of a quality sentence, I share with them what the 6+1 Trait Writing Model of Instruction & Assessment says about sentence fluency: "Sentences vary in length, beginnings, structure, and style, and are so well crafted that the reader moves through the piece with ease" (Education Northwest, 2014). This can involve long and short sentences, and these can be simple, compound, complex, or compound-complex.

So, I start the seventh graders at the beginning of every year with a flipped lesson on sentence structure. I start with compound sentences and we progress through to compound-complex sentences. I give my students four days to complete a flipped lesson on different sentence types. When students finish with each flipped lesson, we do a simple activity of writing an example of each type of sentence on a sentence strip. My students do this with either a partner or as a small group, depending on whether the students truly do understand the concept that is being taught, which I determine from looking at their WSQ assignment. Then, like Anderson, I have posted samples around my room so students can see examples of each type of sentence. However, I want the students to think beyond writing in just formal spaces, but also the informal spaces they write in.

To take the process further and to help students create a resource that they can access outside of school, I have students do two things; first, we work on a collaborative Google Document and then I introduce Twitter. I would like to note that teachers may have some hesitation about using Twitter to help with teaching sentence structure. I discuss this in more depth later, but should say now that it isn't counterproductive at all; students have to not only think about being good digital citizens, but have to carefully think about that space where they have to do their composing within 140 characters.

For example, a student that composes a compound sentence now thinks of an effective way to use a semicolon (middle tweet in Image 4.2) that takes up less characters as a coordinating conjunction, compared to words like *and*, *but*, and *or*. Students have to reflect and think about sentence length and structure. Furthermore, they learn how to communicate effectively and efficiently using social media.

Image 4.2 Sample of one student's Twitter feed with various sentence styles represented

Still, if you are uncomfortable using (or unable to use) Twitter, you can still gain a similar effect using a tool such as a fake Twitter generator (simitator. com/generator/twitter/tweet). Just like I would have students use the fake texting site, they could use this site, too, and take screenshots of their examples.

Also, to fully engage in the process of using social media, when I have my students post to Twitter they utilize the hashtag #fmsgrammar which stands for Fulton Middle School Grammar. It is an easy hashtag for them to remember and we can all follow the #fmsgrammar stream to see many examples.

As these sentences get posted to Twitter, I want my students to be able to understand and do the following:

1. Access the hashtag for examples that will be posted by peers, teachers, and potentially other individuals that want to participate that aren't in our school. These examples can be used in their own writing.
2. Learn how to write in social media spaces more responsibly and see Twitter as a resource, not just another site to inform people they are hanging out with friends or to talk about a TV show.
3. Create a space where there can be positive and intellectual interaction between students by naming the different grammar skills that are being used on the hashtag. See Image 4.3 to see a student identifying the type of sentence that was used.

Students do not have to have a Twitter account, but it is important to communicate with parents about the purpose of using Twitter both in and out of the classroom. At the beginning of the year I send home a permission slip for parents to read over and sign. In addition, this past year, we held a Twitter night in the fall for parents so we could help them see how Twitter can be used as a resource and for them to see examples of what their students are doing. Though we didn't have large number of parents attend our first meeting, we had a second meeting in the spring for parents as well, that was better attended. My principal and I feel that if we can help the parents see how students can use social media in a responsible way, then students will do more than just spout off about their favorite celebrity.

Image 4.3 A student describes her use of a sentence type within a single Tweet

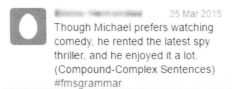

25 Mar 2015
Though Michael prefers watching comedy, he rented the latest spy thriller, and he enjoyed it a lot. (Compound-Complex Sentences) #fmsgrammar

Twitter is one of many social media tools that are available for students to access and use. It is truly amazing the number of social media sites that students are a part of and use on a regular basis. Though there is nothing in the curriculum that states I have to teach my students about digital citizenship or using technology responsibly, I feel it is my duty to help guide them on their journey. Also, when thinking about the Triple E Framework, the Twitter activity can fit under the "Extend" part of the framework where technology is helping to create a bridge between school learning and everyday activities. When it comes to social media, there are many other venues besides Twitter, where our students write.

Sentence Hacking

Prior to the Summer of 2013, I wasn't giving much thought to how students were crafting and creating the different types of sentences. To be honest, I wasn't even thinking about the ways they structured their sentences. That is, I wasn't thinking about it until I had an opportunity to attend the Summer Institute in Digital Literacy at the University of Rhode Island under the direction of Renee Hobbs and Julie Coiro. While there, one of our tasks were to create an artifact to take back to our schools to use in our classrooms that demonstrated the use of technology in a meaningful way.

My partner at the institute, Candace Marcotte, and I decided to work towards creating an artifact that can be used with grammar through multiple units. That is, we designed an activity that isn't just a one-time activity for students, but a tool that they can use to practice the skills throughout the school year. As the week progressed, we came up with an activity I now call "Sentence Hacking:" both because it deals specifically with using sentence combining as a means to play with all types of sentences (compound, complex, and compound-complex), and because we are reorganizing those sentences for various technology-based genres, I like to imply that students are "hacking."

When I start sentence hacking with the students at the beginning of the year, I show them the template (Image 4.4) they will be using by projecting it on the whiteboard (also, a link is available on the wiki under the Chapter 4 resources). Considering the Triple E Framework, I feel that by just modeling this activity, it gets the students motivated to start the learning process with this activity. So, the engagement part isn't difficult. Yet, the extension and enhancements are a little more challenging, but exciting at the same time.

After the students view the template and we go over each online space they write in from day to day, I have the students discuss in groups of four or five which of these spaces they would be more formal in their writing and

Image 4.4 Sentence Hacking Template

the spaces where they can be informal style. A majority of the writing spaces on the template can allow students to be both formal and informal (Facebook, Twitter, E-mail, and text messaging). On the other hand, at the middle school level, I feel it is important for students to identify formal writing skills with word processing, so when they use Google Docs for writing they use formal writing skills. Students should not code switch here and start using their "digitalk" in their Google Doc. In terms of composing an email, this is where students need to differentiate their audience and whether the tone will be formal or informal. This is where we come back as a whole class and together, determine which spaces the students can use their "digitalk." The conversation between me and my students sounded something like this:

Mr. Hyler: Which of these spaces where we write allows us to be flexible with our formal and informal writing skills?
Lydsi: Facebook and Twitter.
Mr. Hyler: Very nice! Are there other spaces where we can go back and forth between formal and informal writing?
MacKenzie: E-mail could be one of those places, depending on who you are emailing.
Mr. Hyler: Can you give me an example?

MacKenzie:	Like if you were emailing a teacher you are not going to use just "u" for the word "you," and we would have to use capital letters and periods.
Mr. Hyler:	Ok, great! What about text messaging? If you are sending a request to Mr. Hyler or to your boss about work you missed, would you use digitalk?
Josh:	You could, but it might get you fired.
Brittany:	It wouldn't get your fired, Josh.
Adam:	It depends on the relationship you had with your boss. If you're friends, it would be okay, but otherwise, you might not want to use it.
Brittany:	It depends on who your teacher is too. I wouldn't do that with Mr. Hyler, but I might with Mrs. Smith.
Mr. Hyler:	Why, because I am the English teacher?
Brittany:	(Laughing) Yes.
Mr. Hyler:	Shouldn't we practice informal and formal writing across all subjects and with everyone?
	There are several nods and pockets of "yes" responses from students around the room.

The above conversation is a huge step for my students to understand how to write in different spaces and so they are aware why it is important to learn these skills. Figure 4.2 shows the results of a similar discussion I had with my first hour eighth grade class. This table is displayed on the whiteboard for students to reference.

It is evident by the end of our conversation that students can clearly determine which spaces they need to be more formal with their writing. However, because students don't practice writing enough in these different spaces (or they write more in one space than the other), they can't always separate the boundaries at times when teachers ask them to turn in a formal writing assignment such as an argumentative essay. That is why I feel this

Figure 4.2 Notes from a class discussion of formality in various digital spaces

Digital Space	Formal/Informal Writing/Both
1. Facebook	1. Both
2. Twitter	2. Both
3. E-mail	3. Formal – Can use informal w/friend
4. Text Messaging	4. Both – More informal
5. Google Document/Word Document	5. Formal
6. Instagram	6. Both

Google Slides activity is important to do with students at least four or five times throughout a nine week marking period.

At the conclusion of our conversation, I use a sentence from *The Giver* by Lois Lowry (the novel we were reading at the time) as mentor text for a compound-complex sentence:

> The fabrics on the upholstered chairs and sofa were slightly thicker and more luxurious; the table legs were not straight like those at home, but slender and curved, with a small carved decoration on the foot.
>
> (p. 74)

Students then take that sentence and use the template to demonstrate the difference between formal and informal writing and to help them practice compound, complex, and compound-complex types of sentences. I give each of the groups the same sentence and ask them to fill in each of the spaces on the template as a group. Though I do this on the whiteboard first with my students, for sake of conversation I have provided an example of a completed template (Image 4.4) after students are given their mentor text from *The Giver* (Lowry, 2006).

This particular group example shows the students using Google Documents and email as a more formal writing space. Formality in email writing is a requirement that I have my students explore because our students have a hard time realizing they need to be more formal with their teachers when asking about grades, missing assignments, or other classroom-related issues. I really like the image the group came up with for Instagram with independent and dependent clauses using the pictograph of the people. The single person represents an independent clause and the multiple people represent dependent clauses. I also like the idea of using visual literacies to meet the needs of those students who are visual learners. A student who doesn't necessarily understand a concept through written words may get a better handle on it through the use of pictures.

Text messaging and Facebook posts are done in more informal ways by the groups, just as they would be more informal in social media. As you can see, they compose similar statements that, although they are informal, capture the idea of what is being said in the original sentence.

I am not surprised by how well my students do with filling out the template and being able to differentiate between the different digital/social platforms. The one platform my students do struggle with is finding pictures to post on Instagram that represents the different types of sentences. It is imperative to have patience if using Instagram within the template. I have adapted my original lesson by now allowing students to take pictures of

Image 4.5 Sentence Hacking with an Example from The Giver

themselves representing the skill if they can't find pictures on the internet. This not only cuts down on time, but allows students to use their phones in meaningful ways and it eliminates copyright infringement. In addition, students could create their own picture using Paint or some other drawing tool. Still, a good place for students to find copyright-free pictures is www.search. creativecommons.org.

Finally, if the template here seems to be too much, remember that other digital tools are available where students can create fake social media entries and texting. Below is a list of some tools to try, one described earlier in this chapter and one which was used in Chapter 3.

◆ simitator.com
◆ faketweetbuilder.com
◆ hclasstools.net/FB/home-page
◆ iphonefaketext.com

Once my students have demonstrated through guided practice that they can fill in the template, I share a Google Documents folder with them, containing numerous templates for them to use on their own when we work on sentence structure. Students are given specific instructions when it is time to move to more independent practice. Below are the directions I put on the projector for my students to follow when they are doing more independent or group practice.

1. Login to your school email account connected to Google.
2. Open the link that Mr. Hyler has posted on the eighth grade page on our website titled "Sentence Structure Template." (This will bring up a blank template similar to the one we have been working on as a class.)
3. Once you click on the link and Google Documents opens, click on the "File" menu.
4. Click on "Make a Copy" in the menu.
5. Rename the copy "YourLastName_Sentence Structure Hack."
6. Start working on the mentor sentence that I have given you from our novel or story.
7. Share your template with Mr. Hyler after you have completed it (template must be completed by the end of our next class period).

From here, students are then asked to look at sentences pulled from mentor texts that we are reading in class. This leads them to using a variety of sentences in their writing and the students are also creating a resource for themselves as they progress through the school year. Furthermore, students are really coming to terms with differentiating their formal and informal writing skills in the various spaces in which they write. The bigger writing assignments that students turn in to me are becoming less riddled with their "digitalk" and they are paying more attention to correct spelling and punctuation. I can confidently say that my middle school students are truly growing as writers.

Putting Lexile Leveling to Use for Writers

Finally, as I think about ways to help my students rewrite simple sentences into more complex ones, I have been playing around with websites like Newsela (newsela.com), Tween Tribune (tweentribune.com), Read Works (www.readworks.org), and News in Levels (www.newsinlevels.com). While we usually think of these sites as ones for reading, I think that they can make great tools for writing, too. To begin, I ask my students to identify an article that they want to read, then set it at a Lexile level below their own. For instance, my seventh graders (who are reading at about 1040) would choose the article at the 830 (fifth grade) level. Then, they identify some sections in the article that they could rewrite. For instance, here is an example from an article about Muhammad Ali, who died as we were working on this chapter ("Newsela | Sports world loses boxing great Muhammad Ali at age 74"), with my own revised versions:

Original Article Text	My Revised Sentences
He was quick with his fists and feet and quick with his mouth, too. Muhammad Ali was a boxing champion who promised to shock the world, and did. He was The Greatest. (830 Level)	Since he was quick with his fists and feet – as well as his mouth – Muhammad Ali promised to shock the world. OR Because he was quick with hands and his mouth, Muhammad Ali was a champion who shocked the world.

Together, we explore a variety of angles to revise the sentence:

- ◆ We notice the simple sentence, even with the conjunctions (ands)
- ◆ We identify and then rethink the use of AWUBIS words: *after, as, although, while, when, until, before, because, if,* and *since*
- ◆ We change the verb connected with Muhammad Ali – he engages in the act of "shocking" rather than promising "to shock"

On the flip side, students might also take a more complex sentence (or sentences) and revise for clarity. Here is an example from one of my students, based on an article about kids who had been in jail (Melamed, 2016), as well as his reflection:

Original Article Text	My Revised Sentences
People like Terrance "T.A" Williams know the law's effect firsthand. He was 17 when he was locked up in adult jail on charges that included robbery and assault.	Terrance "T.A" Williams was 17 when he was first locked up in an adult jail. The charges he had faced were robbery and assault.

I chose to reword these sentences the way I did because it gets rid of all the extra words that were originally in this sentence. Also, because it took out some bigger and more complex words, that if you don't know the definition or meaning to the word you wouldn't know what these sentences are trying to tell you. When you look at all I did was take out some extra detail to get down to the "plain Jane" without all of the extra detail it helps some people understand the sentence better.

No matter the activity, the core of learning about sentences is completely intact. I am simply extending my students' learning into the spaces they are accustomed to writing in on a daily basis. I am continuing to bridge that gap for my students between learning at home and school, breaking down the classroom walls. Again, while the process is engaging, the real value in this particular use of technology comes from enhancing and extending their knowledge of sentence variety and structure.

Next Steps

I always tell my students that I am a geek when it comes to sentences because I like to play around with them and see how they can be constructed. Providing them with play time is crucial for them to understand the makeup of sentences and to see how different parts of sentences can be pieced together. Given the time and tools to work with sentences, the process can be very powerful for students in their understanding of formal and informal writing and they actually see it as being something that is fun. Furthermore, students who show even modest growth have learned valuable skills that they can use in their writing spaces.

Now that students are taking parts of speech and constructing sentences in formal and informal settings, it is time to start thinking about how we can expand our students' vocabulary in a digital world. Students have numerous tools at their disposal that can be used to help them make real-world connections. One of the tools my students used was called Vine, a site for sharing brief videos, but which was taken offline during the production of this book. They now use other means to create videos depicting a real world use of vocabulary words. If real-world connections can be made with vocabulary and spelling, students are sure to retain more of the information they have learned and see the relevance.

5

Enlivening Vocabulary

Somewhere in your social media feeds – or perhaps even a staff meeting – you've probably seen a graphic that shows how reading more and more will, in turn, lead to more vocabulary growth. Neither of us (Troy nor I) are statisticians, but from having a great deal of teaching experience and by watching our own children grow up, we can attest to the ways that vocabulary can continue to grow for students through sustained attention to reading.

More importantly, there are many studies that document the importance of intentional vocabulary study as well as wide exposure to reading. For instance, there are the gaps that emerge early and continue to grow in our students' vocabulary, summarized in what Keith Stanovich coined "the Matthew effect," connecting to the Biblical passage about the rich getting richer and the poor getting poorer (Stanovich, 1986). More recently, the need for disciplinary vocabulary has been developed in research (Shannahan and Shannahan 2008), and we know that teaching students how to recognize words in science, social studies, math, and other subjects matters a great deal.

Of course, the new text complexity standards in the Common Core – which shows a triangle of qualitative and quantitative measures, as well as the influence of the reader himself or herself – make the point about vocabulary study really clear: "Researchers recommend that students be taught to use knowledge of grammar and usage, as well as knowledge of vocabulary, to comprehend complex academic text" (Appendix A, p. 29). Texts are measured, in part, on the vocabulary found within them, often in the form of reading levels or Lexile scores. And, as anyone who has encountered Lexile scores (as a teacher or parent) can attest, while having simple or complicated words does not, in and of itself, make a book, article, or other piece of reading a truly great text, there is no doubt that students must develop their vocabulary over time.

Couple the needs documented in the research with measures of text complexity in the Common Core, and we can see that a reimagined approach to vocabulary instruction is needed. Then, layer on the new SAT because, sadly, what gets measured gets treasured. According to a 2014 article in Time, "The redesigned [SAT] test will focus on deeply understanding more common words rather than being familiar with linguistic gems" (Steinmetz, 2014). Our students need to know the words that they, well, *know*, but in a variety of contexts.

One of those contexts needs to be how they speak and use vocabulary in everyday conversation. "To become word conscious, students first need to develop a feel for how written language is different from everyday conversation" (Texas Reading Initiative, 2002, p. 13). In essence, students need to be conscious about the words they use in their writing and know how different it potentially could be when it is used in the conversations they have with peers and adults.

So, in short, the need to integrate vocabulary instruction with writing instruction is quite necessary. Yet, the challenge in doing so remains as difficult as ever.

The Struggle is Real

I will admit, I have never been a big fan of learning or teaching vocabulary.

For years it seemed that learning vocabulary was the same thing over and over – you learn it just long enough to forget it. And, while I have had my fair share of really great teachers, I can't recall one that helped me make meaningful connections with vocabulary throughout my academic career.

While I don't want to discredit those who taught me, I do know that because of the way vocabulary was taught to me, I have been trying for many years to perfect the way I teach vocabulary to my students. In other words, I want teach better than I was taught.

This can be hard to do for all the reasons I just mentioned above, not to include a list of my own motivations (or lack thereof). Keeping all of that in mind can make teaching vocabulary just as difficult as any other task. Furthermore, I know that teachers, in general, feel like there just isn't enough time to get through everything.

Before we dive into this chapter, I want to begin by sharing a key point from Amy Benjamin and Michael Hugelmeyer. In their book, *Big Skills for the Common Core: Literacy Strategies for the 6–12 Classroom*, Benjamin and

Hugelmeyer have a very short section on how words get learned and stay learned. In this section they write

> Words afford understanding. The understanding that words afford is applicable not only to interpersonal communication, but to thought itself. Words formulate thought, whether the thought turns into speech/writing or not.
>
> (2012, p. 138)

For me, this was a powerful statement because the bottom line is that vocabulary is important for students to be successful communicators, whether through speaking or writing. On a personal note, I think about my own children – nine, seven, and four years old right now – and how many times they ask me what a word means. While I sometimes get just a bit annoyed (c'mon, all the parents out there can admit it!), I generally smile and respond, knowing how important it is for their understanding. It only reinforces for me that vocabulary is a must in my classroom, whether I might like it or not.

So, I want to openly acknowledge that there is a tension in what I do with vocabulary. Other English teachers feel the tension, too, at least the ones that I talk with on a regular basis. As I mentioned above, it seems like we are constantly pressed for time. On the one hand, you already know that I am really against the idea of "drill and kill" – I want my students to learn things thoroughly and thoughtfully. On the other hand, I am trying to cover lots of material, especially with new vocabulary, and I do worry that students will be overwhelmed.

Oftentimes, even with the best of intentions, vocabulary can overtake a lesson. For instance, there are those teachable moments when a student asks the meaning of a word and – though I intend to spend no more than three or four minutes going over the word – it may take more like ten minutes, or longer. Going over the different types of words, my students and I often get engrossed in conversation. When I think about those moments, I have to reflect back on what Benjamin and Hugelmeyer said and realize that words formulate thought, and that what I do with vocabulary is important.

Thus, I live with this tension. While some of my English teaching colleagues might think that I am betraying a more natural approach, allowing students to discover words in context and create their own lists for vocabulary, I am trying to balance all of the factors noted above, especially our perpetual lack of time. Even in their writing, I can't always find the evidence that they really have the words memorized and are able to use them as part of their working vocabulary unless I ask students to do some of the activities described later in this chapter.

So, before I start having people light the torches and sharpen the pitch-forks, I fully recognize that some of the exercises described in the rest of the chapter are dangerously close to the dreaded "drill and kill" exercises that, as I already mentioned, I don't like and many educators shy away from. Still, I hope that you will see how I try to provide a variety and balance of activities for my students, enriched with technology tools.

Building Vocabulary with Quizlet

Again, I struggle with finding that balance in the 60 minutes I have to instruct my students each day and then allow them to work. While it feels like a para-dox, I try to do the best for my seventh graders as they enter into the middle school world. I am also not simply using technology for its own sake, merely "engaging" them for sense of engagement as the lower levels of the Triple E Framework indicate. The seventh graders are trying to find balance them-selves and, with Quizlet, I feel that I am helping ease their stress and showing them the path for using technology in meaningful, purposeful ways. I just keep telling myself that vocabulary matters for them as readers, writers, and speakers, as well as for them as thoughtful, deliberate citizens, even if we are sometimes just using virtual flashcards.

Troy and I introduced Quizlet in our first book, *Create, Compose, Connect!*. There, I briefly mentioned it as a tool for students to create online flashcards. Quite simply, I thought, Quizlet could only be used for that, nothing more. Over the past few years I have had the chance to explore the tool in more depth, and there are many features to Quizlet that I did not go into in our first book; my students and I have found many of the features helpful and applicable in and out of the classroom. Here is how we do the work.

Building "Study Sets" in Quizlet

Because it is such a useful tool, I show Quizlet to my seventh graders at the beginning of the year. While my students are learning the ropes of how Mr. Hyler works and how middle school is going to be for them, I want them to have a positive experience and I don't want to overwhelm them. Thus, I make it clear to them that I have three goals when they use Quizlet for vocabulary.

1. I want students to see that there are valuable tools and apps that can be used on their phone or tablets, sometimes for just a few minutes at a time, and that they can truly create an "anytime, anyplace" environment for learning. Again, the tech should enhance and extend, not just engage alone.

2. Because of this, students can study without the excuse of, "I didn't have my flashcards," or "I lost my flashcards." As they learn vocabulary in their own day-to-day lives, they can add it to their Quizlet decks.

3. To build on this just a bit more, vocabulary isn't just something that is done for a given time period and forgotten. It is valuable for building their own knowledge and ultimately making them more robust speakers, readers, and writers.

Quizlet takes me approximately two class periods to go over with my seventh graders. Rather than using the term "flashcard," Quizlet allows you to build "study sets," though I still call them flashcards with my students. While it could appear that this is valuable instruction time lost, it is not; as we go through the features of Quizlet, I am working with current vocabulary lists from our readings to build our first deck of flashcards. Students go to the website and sign-up, and then I show them the basics of how to create a set of flashcards for studying. Also, I show them how they can create folders where they can put multiple sets of flashcards they have created. Image 5.1 shows what the left-hand of the home screen looks like for a typical student. Here, we have captured the student's work "as is," so please be considerate of the spelling mistake with "Sleepy Hollow."

Image 5.1 Student View of Quizlet Interface and Study Sets Created

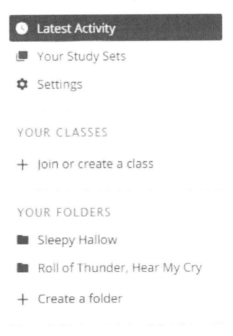

Quizlet has many useful and rewarding features that can accommodate many different types of learners. This, of course, hits on the "Engagement" level of the Triple E Framework. First, besides helping all students not lose their flashcards because they are stored in the student's Quizlet account, I can create sets for Quizlet which also has a feature where they can do spelling practice. Students choose the "Speller" option at the top of the screen after they have chosen one of their sets (See Image 5.2, which points out these different options).

When students begin, a voice will say the words from their flashcards and students must then write out the word correctly. While I do not do just spelling tests, the fact that they must spell is a great feature because I do require my students to know how to spell the word on top of knowing the definition. I deem it important for students to still learn the spelling of new words so the likelihood of them using new words in their writing increases.

One of the other great features of Quizlet site is the games that the students can play using the sets that they have created. I like this feature for a few reasons. At one level, it brings in the gamers in my room and they are more engaged than if just creating flashcards and forgetting about them. I won't explain the games in great detail, but the Scatter game is essentially a matching game and the Gravity game is like the classic Asteroids game. At another level, even for my non-gamers, these options offer my students variety. Yet, the options don't end there.

As noted above, Quizlet can meet the needs of many different learners. More specifically, it has great features for special education students and those with lower literacy levels. The voice feature helps those students that may have trouble pronouncing words. Hearing the words spoken can help them develop study habits that can make them successful. Furthermore, students who may not get support outside of school can benefit from this tool because those students who have mobile devices can access the mobile app and can use the different features to help them study.

Using Quizlet also fits into how I follow the Triple E Framework in terms of extending student learning beyond the classroom walls. To ensure that the

Image 5.2 Tools in the Quizlet App

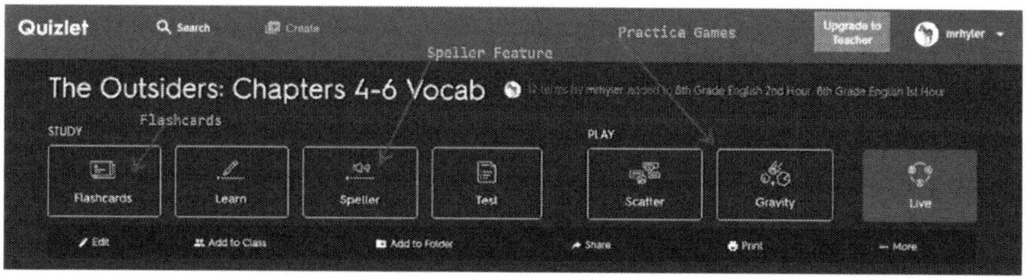

students are actually making the flashcards and attempting to use the site as an effective study tool, I have my students share a link to their flashcards; then, I give them a formative assessment grade of anywhere between five to ten points. If students don't complete the assignment outside of class, I have them complete it in class.

Building Toward Assessment with Quizlet

The pitchforks and torches may not be coming out yet, but I have feeling you might get them out in this section . . .

Still, I do have to say that there are some places in school for "traditional" notions of assessment and accountability. Because my seventh graders are new to the middle school experience, one of the priorities we have as a staff is to teach them responsibility. With that being said, I have my seventh graders take a quiz over their vocabulary terms. Sometimes the quiz is over individual chapters or over two or three chapters. It really does depend on the number of words or the chapter(s) we are doing in our reading. For example, I give my students a list of fifteen words for the first three chapters of *The Outsiders*. The students have access to the words through the "class" I have created on Quizlet. Their job is to make a copy of the list for their own study set and complete the list by adding the definitions. Then, students share the list with me via email so I can make sure the list is complete. Typically, with fifteen words, I will give students a formative assessment grade where I give them half a point for each word and half a point for the definition. From there, the students will then take a traditional quiz and apply the words to their own writing. For instance, here is one of the lists from *The Outsiders*.

asset	elite	rebellious	souped-up	vaguely
buckskin	hitched	reeling	stalked	
cowlick	madras	roguishly	suspicious	

I try to mix things up and give them matching on some quizzes and fill in the blank on others. In this case, I have already created study sets in Quizlet and I can distribute them to my students directly through the Quizlet app or website. I believe I am creating a scaffold for my seventh graders when it comes to trying to help them better understand the content I am teaching them. My students really enjoy Quizlet and find it very beneficial. The seventh graders are taking those small steps to help them get better acclimated to middle school curriculum while using technology in smart and responsible ways.

Later in this chapter, when I discuss the videos that my eighth graders create, I will go into detail about how students apply the vocabulary terms to their writing, but I will mention it briefly here as well. With seventh graders, I have to be more specific in showing them how to have them use the new words they are learning in their writing. There are two options for helping seventh graders in this situation.

First, depending on a school's cell phone policy, students could have their phones out next to their laptops with the Quizlet app open to the vocabulary terms where they can see the definitions and the words. Second, it could be a really good time to teach students how to have two tabs open on their computer so they can see both pages at the same time where they can go back and forth between their writing and Quizlet where their vocabulary words are housed.

There is no doubt about it, time and patience are both crucial with seventh grade, and anyone who has taught seventh grade knows this fact all too well. I require my seventh graders to include anywhere from five to seven words in their formal writing assignment that they do during our units of study. Similar to what eighth graders do, I have them highlight the words they use throughout their Google Doc and they are graded in a summative manner on the correct and effective use of the vocabulary words.

Extensions for Quizlet

In terms of extending the use of Quizlet and the idea of students studying their vocabulary, there are a few ideas that can potentially lead to more students being successful. I feel Quizlet is something that can assist students bridging their learning from school to their everyday lives by allowing them to study and practice vocabulary that they could, potentially, use in their different social circles such as friends, family, or future employers. For example, though they are terms not commonly used today, I often hear students using the terms "green around the gills" and "heater" after those terms are introduced. Of course by effectively building their vocabulary skills they can also apply their enhanced vocabulary to emails, formal papers, or even Facebook posts. These different writing spaces allow them to practice new vocabulary and help build confidence in their effective use of new words.

As students use Quizlet throughout the year, it can also be a valuable tool for other classrooms such as Social Studies or Science. Those two core subjects alone have a tremendous amount of important vocabulary for students to study and know. Furthermore, I can see Quizlet as great tool for foreign language classes where students are learning new adjectives or nouns in Spanish or French. Even helping ESL (English as a Second Language) students could benefit. I envision ESL students being able to carry a tablet from class to class or even use their cell phones where they can access words on the Quizlet app to help assist them in the areas where they have trouble translating. It can even be a tool used to help with other lessons and activities involving vocabulary that aren't just about taking a quiz, as we will discuss in the next section.

Breathing Life into Vocabulary with Video

As I mentioned in the introduction to this chapter, we can't just expect students to regurgitate vocabulary terms by learning to spell them and giving the correct definitions.

Students are going to remember a word just long enough to do well on a quiz or a test . . . and then forget about it. Moreover, there will be the resistant students who are going to look at vocabulary instruction and assignments as just one more thing to do. While passing the SAT is not the only reason that we would want students to have a deep, nuanced understanding of any single vocabulary word, the fact that they need to look at a relatively familiar word from a variety of different perspectives on that test (and in life) makes a deeper dive into vocabulary an important task.

So, I wanted to know how I could engage as many of my students in vocabulary study as possible while making the skills they learn applicable to what they do inside and outside of school. "Students remember more when they relate new information to known information, transforming it in their own words, generating examples and non-examples, producing antonyms and synonyms, and so forth" (Texas Reading Initiative, 2002, p. 18). Thus, I created a lesson where my eighth grade students could create a video showing real-world application of the vocabulary I was asking them study in class.

I started using this lesson two years ago and – at the time – had my students using Vine (vine.co), an app where students could create short, six-second videos and post them on a Twitter account or send links to their friends. I figured that Vine was a simple way to make a very focused, simple video. In fact, I often had my seventh graders make Vines until it was taken offline.

However, with the eighth graders, we have moved on to another video-making platform, WeVideo (wevideo.com). One reason I decided to let my students do this is because I felt Vine was limiting my students when it came to them being creative with their videos. In addition, I felt that the videos aren't long enough for their audience to truly grasp what the students were trying to do (or, for that matter, for them to fully express their ideas).

WeVideo's interface is fairly straight-forward, and I am also open to the students using other video apps they may find useful. In fact, I do have some students go above and beyond with other platforms like iMovie. In this section, however, I will be focusing on what my eighth grade students created with WeVideo because of the amount of success I have had with the activity and the platform. Examples of student videos are available on the wiki under the Chapter 5 link.

The Vocabulary Video Assignment

In my classroom, we study vocabulary most intently during our reading units. When reading novels such as *The Outsiders*, vocabulary is crucial for students' understanding of the 1960s, an era not *that* long ago, but still quite a foreign time for my students. Words such as "Madras cloth," "savvy," "reckon," "the fuzz," and "heater" all have distinct meanings in the book.

I start by introducing a list of vocabulary terms to my students that typically consists of no more than 15–20 words. This isn't the only set of terms that they receive, especially with a novel, and they may examine three or four lists throughout a novel. Each student gets a copy of the list of words and I post a copy of the words to my website so they can keep a digital copy of the vocabulary we do throughout the year in their Google Drive.

As a class, we go through the list and discuss the meaning of each word as it applies to the text we are reading (later in the chapter, I will discuss an extension students can do with words that have more than one meaning and can be used as different parts of speech). When we are done going over the list, I have my students break up into pairs or triads. After giving the students a few minutes to get organized with their partner, I begin introducing the assignment and the requirements. Each pair of students are responsible for doing two words and, in some cases, a group may get lucky and have just one word. If this does happen, I don't change the requirements for that group; instead, I let that group know I have higher expectations for them when it comes to their video because they do only have one word.

I begin by telling the students that they need to create a video that is at least one to three minutes long. As I have mentioned before, I have used Vine in the past, but I really feel that six seconds is not long enough for this particular assignment. At the beginning of the video, I want them to present the word with the definition as it is being used in the novel we are doing. Students will need to have their novels handy so they can go back and look at the word in context. I always feel it is very important to give all the tools necessary for my students to be successful.

When it comes to the making of the videos, many students either will embed the word and definition on the screen or they will write it out on a piece of paper and display it at the beginning of their video. I tend not to be picky when it comes to this, but I do nudge my students to be more creative than just holding up a piece of paper in front of the camera when they are recording.

The definition has been displayed in a caption-style template in Image 5.3. Not every student used a banner similar to the student example below, but using the banner is ideal and it can be brought back into the video towards the end to remind the students of the definition just as I like them to do.

I give my students three days to produce the video. This gives time for students to do the video outside of class and to use WeVideo to edit their video. When students are wrapping up the video, I do ask them to put the word and definition at the end of their video, too. This gives the audience a reminder of what the words and definitions are and it adds a closer to the video. The assignment guideline sheets available on the companion wiki.

In addition to the definition, students know I want them to create a video that shows the definition being used in a real life situation. For instance, if students were using the vocabulary term "treachery" (Image 5.4) from *The Outsiders*, they might create a video of a fake bank robbery where the one of the bank robber performs "treachery" on his partners in crime; students could potentially use the term in some dialogue that is spoken during the video that was created by the students. (Just as a side note, students would have to use paper guns that they have made or create the video at home so

Image 5.3 Definition displayed in a caption in WeVideo

Image 5.4 A Student Enacts the Idea of "Treachery" in a Video

that they don't get in trouble with even fake guns at school.) If the students created the video outside of school, I encourage them to use paintball guns or airsoft guns in this instance.

Before the students even begin talking about what they want to do, I tell them that I want to see a plan, and, thus, ask my students to create a storyboard (we've included links to a few of our favorite storyboards on the wiki). The storyboard must be approved by me before students can begin production and I tell the students that they may have to use more than just six boxes. Typically, students can put together a storyboard in about 30 minutes and bring me the storyboards during class for my approval. I am looking for them to show me they will display the word and definition at the beginning and end. Moreover, I look at their video to see if it is actually going to show the appropriate meaning of the word from the context of the book, and it will make sense to their audience of classmates. The video also allows students to share alternate definitions of the word as well.

When their storyboards are approved, I have them begin video production. After they complete their videos, I have them turn the videos in by emailing me their entire video file or a link to their video, depending on where and how the students produced their video. Grading the videos, for me, is more formative than it is summative. I do however, want to honor my students' time and make sure they do have a clear understanding of the word and how it is being used. I don't get too complicated with the grading. The students get 20 points for their video based on the categories in Figure 5.1.

Figure 5.1 Evaluation Categories for the Vocabulary Videos

Planning – Storyboard – 5 pts	Storyboard reflects word and definition being used at the beginning and end of the video and video will accurately demonstrate the correct use of the word according how it was used in the novel.
Drafting – Video Production – 10 pts	Video displays word and definition at the beginning and end of the video and depicts the correct use of the word as it appeared in the book. Everyone played a role in creating the video whether they were in the video, created something for the video or was the person recording the video.
Connections – 5 pts	What is the connection to the text we are reading? For example, how does the word relate to the short story *The Outsiders*? Why do you think the author made that word choice where it is located in the text?
Evaluating/ Reflection – 5 pts	After watching the video as a class, group participants wrote a short 3–4 line sentence reflection about how well they felt the production of the video went, the challenges they had with their particular vocabulary word, and what they could have done differently, if anything. I also ask them to reflect on their new understanding of the vocabulary word (and its meaning in the context of the book).

Also, the students have a short reflection that they need to write at the conclusion of their video. I take a day at the end of the week that we do the video, typically Friday, and we watch the videos that were produced. As we watch each video, I ask the group whose video is on display to watch and listen how their classmates react; they must ask themselves if their audience fully understands the word and its definition. In other words, they must imagine whether each of their classmates could use the word in their writing correctly and effectively.

As the video is playing, the other students have their laptops and are writing the definitions in their Quizlet lists that they have started. By the time the videos are done, everyone has a completed list to study.

After I have shown each video, I then have all students complete their short reflection within their online journal they created at the beginning of the year. Their online journals have already been shared with me via Google Docs, so it is just a matter of me checking what they wrote. I want my students to think about the process they went through with the video and how they can apply those skills to their own writing in the near future. Here is an example of an eighth grade student reflection after the vocabulary video project was done.

Creating the video was a lot of fun, it was better than doing a worksheet or crossword puzzle. The only time the video was hard to do is when we couldn't find a time to meet after school. I felt I learned the word better because I was actually doing something with the word and not staring at it on a piece of paper, it stuck with me more. If Mr. Hyler gave us a chance to make the videos over, I would make sure the sound was better on our video, it kind of sucked. – Josh

From here, the students know they are not done with their vocabulary. They know that I am not going to just forget about what they did. During our unit on *The Outsiders*, my students are thinking about the characters who are in the novel. One of the first questions I ask them at the beginning of the book, when all of the characters are introduced, is who they think they are most closely related to. I ask this particular question because, at the end of the novel, my students are writing a compare/contrast paper that is about the major characters in the story. While students are writing this paper, they need to use a minimum of five vocabulary words from each set they get through the novel. So, overall, they will use around fifteen new words. As mentioned before, the students are recording definitions of vocabulary terms as they are watching the videos that have been made.

I want to point out that I do not require my students to stick to the exact definition of how the word was used in the book (though they do need to demonstrate that they understand that usage, too). I actually encourage it because I feel that it gives the students more freedom to learn. Oftentimes, students will raise their hands while working on vocabulary videos asking me to clarify if the word is used as a noun or a verb. I respond by asking them to look at how the word is used and confidently decide for themselves. Then, I ask them to think about how the word changes or a specific passage changes if the word was used differently in terms of the parts of speech. They may stray, if you will, and use the word as a verb instead of an adjective where it may be possible and that is perfectly fine with me for this particular project.

When it comes to grading, the students' writing assignments are where I am grading them in a summative manner. They get one point for using each word correctly. So that I can easily see where they have put their vocabulary words, I have the students highlight them in their Google Document with a designated color. In the next section, I will discuss where students can extend their thinking beyond just creating the video and using the words in their writing.

Extensions and Adaptations

When I think about vocabulary instruction and how I did it in the past, I was always glued to that one, single meaning of the word for my students. I feel as if I had blinders on to what my students could actually accomplish with vocabulary. Now, I want my students to explore vocabulary, not feel restricted in what they are doing. I honestly believe that if students feel restricted in what they are doing, they are not going to take an interest in the assignments they are writing or they won't take ownership of their work. Since doing the videos for vocabulary, I am having more and more students asking about the multiple definitions of words they are learning.

In addition, they are asking if they can create a separate (or longer) video that includes the other definitions to the words. This gets me really excited as their teacher because they want to explore more and play around more with the words. From here, I can make some really great connections for both my seventh and eighth grade. Furthermore, the extensions I want my students to create fit into the Triple E Framework because students are continuing to use their devices in responsible ways outside of the classroom. Also, it enhances their learning by creating more scaffolds for more complex assessments later such as their writing assignments or standardized tests.

Another extension that could be used connects with my seventh graders completing a flipped lesson on synonyms and antonyms. I see this as a great place to make connections for my seventh graders and have them look at current vocabulary terms and to see where they could find antonyms and synonyms of the words they are using. A simple whole-class activity such as sharing a grid on a Google Document similar to Figure 5.2 can be done in less than half of one class period. From here, I tell students to find their own box with one of the vocabulary words and try and find a synonym or an antonym for the word.

If students are unable to find a synonym or an antonym, I challenge them to think about the different definition a word might have and why the word might change from an adjective to a verb or a noun. As an extension, students could add the part of speech in the table. Furthermore, students could learn the origins of the words to potentially help with future spelling or pronunciation of words.

One of the other ways you could help with retention is to dedicate a page on your classroom website that is just vocabulary that has been learned throughout the year. This could include anything from creating a series of lists, creating links, or creating word clouds.

Figure 5.2 Synonyms and Antonyms List for Seventh Grade Vocabulary Lesson

conspicuous	dwindle	frantically	timid
S – eminent	S – decrease	S – berserk	S – afraid
A – vague	A – enhance	A – calmly	A – bold
tranquil	acquainted	sensational	gaunt
S – sedative	S – enlightened	S – amazing	S – lean
A – turbulent	A – ignorant	A – inferior	A – thick
skulked	sauntered	stolid	
S – evade	S – sashay	S – heavy	
A – encounter	A – rush	A – aware	

Word clouds can also be used as an extension activity for students. Word clouds can be built using:

◆ Wordle (www.wordle.net)
◆ Tagxedo (www.tagxedo.com)
◆ Tagul (tagul.com)
◆ WordCram (wordcram.org)
◆ Wordsalad (wordsaladapp.com – app for both iOS and Android)

Word clouds can help students build word associations with the new words that they have learned. Then, they can apply it to their writing. I see this as being a great pre-writing activity for students. This is a great vocabulary exercise for my eighth grade students when they are writing their memoirs and they have to include dialogue and my seventh graders can do this activity before they write their myths.

To quickly explain this activity, students would take a word such as "said," then I would have them use the website Thesaurus.com and plug in the word to see what additional words they could use to replace it in the dialogue tags that they write. Students will see synonyms to that word and then plug them into Tagul.com and create a word cloud similar to Image 5.6. I direct my students to choose words they know they would use in their writing, not just any word they might think sounds cool. Many teachers call these "dead words," as do I. In order for students to show the term "said" is at the heart of finding replacement synonyms, they need to type that word in more times to Tagul in order for it to pop up in the middle as in Image 5.5.

Image 5.5 A Word Cloud for Alternatives to the Word "Said"

So, as you can see, the word "said" is bigger because that is the word the students started with and is the most over-used. They are trying to find other synonyms that are associated with that word. The students can take a screenshot of the word cloud and put it into their vocabulary folder they created in Google Documents and refer to the word cloud when they are doing their specific writing assignment.

Student Vocabulary Growth Over Time

As my students work through vocabulary throughout the year, I enjoy seeing not only how they grow with their uses of vocabulary, but I also am thrilled to see the creativity that comes out of them when they are using technology in meaningful and productive ways.

One of the first and most prevalent changes that I see in my students is the simple fact they are getting away from the use of "dead" words. Because sixth grade is still in our elementary building, seventh graders are coming to me at the beginning of the year using words such as *said, bad, happy*, and other similar "dead" words. Because I want them to become middle school writers, I have to force them get away from the words that they used at the elementary level. In addition, with the various vocabulary exercises we do in class, I see my students retaining more words and thinking about them in more critical ways besides just memorizing them and forgetting them.

Furthermore, students are applying the words that they are learning – in their next essay, they highlight the words in Google Docs. As I mentioned earlier, it shows me that they are, in fact, actually using the word. Moreover, let's face it, this makes grading a lot easier, at least on that one element of word choice.

I am still trying to find a balance. I am always on the lookout for other assessment strategies that we could or should use with vocabulary. Sometimes it is as simple as just giving students repeated exposure to grade level words and text, or simply playing a game on Quizlet or some other site that can offer vocabulary review. No matter what approach is taken with vocabulary, it is important, and students do need to be doing it throughout the year. There is more to it than "drill and kill" with students. Now with our state switching to the SAT instead of the ACT as form of assessment for juniors, it has become even more important for me as an eighth grade teacher to help my students develop a solid vocabulary.

Next Steps

Vocabulary deserves our attention as teachers, and students need to see how it is applicable to life as a student and as an individual. After all, they are middle school students, and if we can't help them make those connections we aren't engaging them as learners.

Over the past several years I have been focusing more on purposeful vocabulary instruction. Recently, it came to my attention that by the time students reach high school, they should know anywhere between 60,000 to 100,000 vocabulary terms. That is not an unrealistic number if the conscious effort is made to implement it into daily lessons and units.

I know vocabulary instruction is being stressed more and more, but as Troy and I have been trying to show, traditional instruction – where students are "drilled" then "killed" – isn't going to make new vocabulary terms "stick" with our students. As mentioned before, they will remember the word just long enough to do well on a quiz or a test.

So, by giving students opportunities to use new words purposefully through formal writing assignments or through speaking opportunities, and by allowing them to create videos where they can practice the words in social settings, students will not only be more likely to remember the words they are playing with, they will know how to use them in different contexts. By adding in a simple study tool such as Quizlet, students not only have the support inside and outside of school, but they are learning while playing games.

Grammar can't always be fun and games, but as educators we can make it more engaging. In Chapter 6 we will explore how students can make more conscious moves with punctuation and, in addition, help them to remember capitalization rules.

6

Mastering Mechanics: Capitalization and Punctuation

The first thing that I think about when it comes to capitalization and punctuation is cellphones. Why?

My thoughts float first to phones because we all have either seen students send – or we have sent ourselves – text messages where capital letters were missing or punctuation has been incorrect, especially in the age before autocorrect.

My thoughts then shift immediately to this: how can I correct this behavior in my students when they are making some of these same errors in their formal writing assignments that they hand in to me throughout the year? Of course, I am not looking to rip the cellphone out of their hand and pass out worksheets! As Troy and I mentioned at the beginning of the book, educators can't completely blame technology for the habits that have been formed by the students that walk our hallways. After all, I know I am guilty at times sending some of those same types of messages to my friends and family.

The challenge – and opportunity – then, is getting our students to separate the times when they are supposed to use proper mechanics while writing formally from the times when it is more acceptable to send "u" to their friends.

We can teach the rules of capitalization and punctuation over and over again – and correct those same errors in their essays – but our students are still going to forget some of the rules. Also, they might make the frequent mistake of not putting the comma in the right place simply due to the fact that they have not had enough writing practice. In my opinion, by the time my students reach me, punctuation and capitalization should be a review, but it isn't . . . it is an ongoing process that we need to continue to coach them through over the course of their academic careers.

For instance, one brief example I can share from my own classroom is during the cross-curricular Civil War unit. Because many of the eighth graders might have only heard of the Civil War, but have not necessarily immersed themselves in the subject matter, they may have a hard time forming the habit of capitalizing the words "civil" and "war," at least when used as a proper noun referring to a significant event in American history. Yes, I know students *should* know that proper nouns are capitalized, but unless they are frequently studying wars, they aren't accustomed to capitalizing such words.

I don't want to get ahead of myself before we address specific lessons and skills surrounding capitalization and punctuation, but I think it is important to point out some items and ideas. First, there is a difference between students using a computer to type their formal writing assignments and them using their phones to text a friend. However, more and more students are accessing their assignments on devices to complete their work. Lisa Nielsen, author and blogger, writes in her blog *The Innovative Educator* that, in February of 2013, "39% of middle school students use smartphones for homework . . . [and] 31% of middle school students say they use a tablet for homework." At the time of this writing, those statistics are nearly four years old, and back then more than a third of students are using their devices to complete homework. I would venture to say that it may be close to 50%, if not higher, today.

And, yes, we realize that there is still a gap – the digital divide. Some students have always-on access in their pockets; many do not. Still, as of April 2015, Amanda Lenhart of the Pew Internet and American Life Project reported that "Nearly three-quarters of teens have or have access to a smartphone and 30% have a basic phone, while just 12% of teens 13–17 say they have no cellphone of any type." Again, we know that it isn't perfect, but teachers need to face the facts that most of their students have devices and are using them on a daily basis.

So, I wonder, could this be one of the reasons students are having difficulty with capitalization and punctuation in their writing? I don't know if that is all of the story. As much as Troy and I both advocate the use of technology, we know that it doesn't solve all our problems. Put another way, Gerald Graff and Cathy Birkenstein, known for their academic text *They Say, I Say: The Moves That Matter in Academic Writing*, proclaim that student use of technology as not necessarily the cause, or the cure, of students' writing problems:

As for how these digital technologies have influenced student writing, our own view, based on the writing we have seen in our combined seventy years of teaching, is that this influence is neither disastrous, as the critics fear, nor wonderfully revolutionary, as the proponents claim.

(p. 170–171)

Graff and Birkenstein's neutral stance on technology shows they see the bigger picture with students. Yes, technologies are influencing our students, but not to the point we need to be so concerned that we don't address the bigger picture. Perhaps saying that we, as teachers, need to still teach grammar by allowing – in fact, inviting – our students to use technology in responsible ways. This is the stance we have taken in all our work, and will continue to share in this next section.

Capitalization

With this topic, I want to highlight just a few activities that have helped my students become better at remembering capitalization in their own writing, even in an era of autocorrect.

To start, I am going to refer to Jeff Anderson's book, *Mechanically Inclined*, once again. In Chapter 3, Anderson discusses how he shares the seven capitalization rules with his students over several days before holding them accountable for these rules in their writing. He goes through the rules with examples and then posts the rules on his wall in the classroom similar to the rules listed below.

Though I love Anderson's approach to the subject matter, I have not found this particular approach to be the most effective for my own students; instead, I am looking for the capitalization rules to stick and not be forgotten the next day in class. When I read my students' writing, I am often looking for areas of concern and for that reason I have them highlight areas of what they feel is correct grammar use. For example, I have students highlight two to three complex sentences to demonstrate they can use them correctly. Furthermore, grammar concepts such as commas and capitalizing the pronoun "I" are easy areas for me to identify where students need work. The trend I often notice with seventh graders is transitioning from elementary grades where using more simple sentences in their writing is appropriate; now, I want them to use a variety of sentences to increase the complexity of their writing to demonstrate they are becoming more like middle school writers and moving away from their elementary ways of writing. The trends in eighth grade are more about students stepping out of their comfort zone and trying new punctuation such as the semicolon or colon. Then, I shift my lessons to help them write transition sentences instead of just using one word to transition from paragraph to paragraph. For example: first, second, third, next, etc. For me, it is time to turn my attention towards preparing them for high school. Each grade level poses new and exciting challenges for middle school writers that can easily be tackled head on.

As middle school students approach these challenges, technology can support them. Because I am putting students at the center of the activity and taking the steps to be a part of their everyday lives where they spend time writing, I again try to move from the "Engagement" level of the Triple E Framework into the "Enhance" and "Extend" levels. I try to stay conscious of the technologies my students are using. By keeping students at the center and using different digital tools to engage students while helping them retain what they are learning, I am showing how technology can be integrated responsibly into the classroom. Technology can help bridge the disconnect students have when it comes to writing in formal and informal spaces. It isn't that students don't want to use correct grammar such as capitalization and punctuation, it is simply that they don't know how. Once students can differentiate between the two, that bridge will be built and they will be able to effectively work through the different writing spaces as well as adapt the grammar lessons they have learned to their writing, especially with capitalization and grammar concepts.

So, what I do is start by having my students' replicate a chart (see below) similar to what Anderson has put in his classroom. Similar to what I described in earlier chapters, the chart my students create looks more like a table and is put in their grammar guide in Google Docs for easy access anywhere they may be. Besides having the convenience of being digital, my students only write down the problem areas we have seen together in their writing. This does not mean the other rules are not discussed, but it does give students more of a focus for their writing. Figure 6.1 below is something that my students complete throughout the year, and this is a snapshot through the end of the first semester.

Capitalization Rules

1. Proper nouns
   ◆ (Fulton Middle School, Middleton, Jeremy)
2. Proper adjectives
   ◆ (English muffin, Sony television, Chinese food)

3. Title with a last name

   ◆ (Coach **H**yler, **P**resident **O**bama)

4. First word in a direct quotation

   ◆ (Vanessa asked, "**W**hat can I write about?")

5. Titles

   ◆ (**T**he **O**utsiders, **H**oot, **T**een **I**nk)

6. Letter openings

   ◆ (**D**ear **M**r. Hicks,)

7. First word of a letter closing

   ◆ (**Y**ours truly,)

At the beginning of the year I require my students to write a formal email, hence the emphasis on the opening and closing of a letter (guidelines for this assignment are on the companion wiki that accompanies the book). As a staff, we decided that it was necessary to address how to write a formal email because too many times students were emailing the teachers as if they were emailing their BFFs.

Thus, we want to teach them, in terms of life skills, how to formally address teachers, principals, paraprofessionals, and other school staff when they are inquiring about their homework, missing assignments, times they

Figure 6.1 Student Sample of Capitalization Rules

Capitalization Rule	Punctuation Rule	Example	Student's Words
1. Letter Opening	Comma or Colon	Dear Mr. Hyler, To Whom it May Concern:	There has to be a comma after the opening if you know the person. When writing to someone you don't know, use a colon.
2. Closing of a letter	Comma	Your Student,	There must be a comma at the end of the closing before you sign your name.
3. Proper Nouns	N/A	Fulton, Ford, John Deere, Middleton	All proper nouns need to be capitalized.
4. Pronoun "I"	N/A	Josh and I went to the football game Friday.	When "I" stands alone, you have to capitalize it.

are absent, and other matters. By having students complete this task, we start the year addressing the difference between formal and informal writing as well as who their audience is when they are writing. Capitalization and punctuation become an issue because students often don't pause to think about who they are emailing. Thus, I feel the issues in Figure 6.1 are important for students to consider.

It is evident that one of the biggest differences between what Anderson has on his chart and what my students manage with their digital devices is the proper noun "I." Over the past few years, this has become one of the biggest issues in my students' writing, and one I will take up below. When students are initially done with the assignment at the beginning of the year, we as teachers see a significant improvement when it comes to issues like capitalization and punctuation. I have been stopped several times in the hall by our middle school teachers about how beautiful the students' emails look since completing the assignment. I say this not to brag, but to show how important it is that the students learn the necessary skills that can be used both inside and outside of school.

The Dreaded Pronoun: "i"

Over the last few years I have had the privilege of speaking to dozens of language arts teachers at various professional development events and they all have expressed they have the same issue with our favorite first-person pronoun: I. Or, as we often see it: i.

Earlier in the chapter, I discussed how students will whine about not using Word. Well, this is one of those small problems we face as teachers. If students are accustomed to Word, they will struggle with capitalizing "I" because, well, Word does it for them. Though this may pose a small challenge, it can easily be fixed. Now, I am not going to claim I have the magic solution to this dilemma that plagues us as we are grading our students' papers, but I have found something that has helped a great deal as students are editing their writing.

So, there is a wonderful, but simple tool that both Word and Google Docs have that has not only helped my students do a better job of capitalizing the pronoun "I," but it has also introduced them to using the feature for other searches in their writing: the "find" feature. If students hit Control+F on their keyboards (Command+F on a Mac), a box will appear in the upper right-hand corner, as in Image 6.1. Alternatively, the "Find" feature is listed under the "Edit" menu.

If students type in the letter "I" and then hit a space (as shown in Image 6.2), all of the "i" characters that stand alone will be highlighted throughout their

Image 6.1 The "Find" Search Box in Google Docs

writing and students can go through and fix any that they may not have capitalized in their writing. Before students even begin to think about sharing their writing with me for grading, as a whole class, I have my students complete this search so they can find, and fix, the mistakes they may have made. It takes five to seven minutes and saves me a huge headache when it comes to grading. Students love this simple feature and, as the year progresses, I notice my students using it for other areas of their writing. For example, the seventh graders can use it right away when they are writing their formal emails (Image 6.2).

In a similar manner, when my eighth graders do their Civil War research paper they can type in the words "Civil" and "War" and go through and capitalize the proper noun. By the second semester, there is barely any prompting by me to use the find feature, and students' writing has improved greatly in this area.

There is also the option for "Find and Replace," which does save them some time if there are many errors. This feature is more easily accessed under the "Edit" menu as compared to using keystrokes, at least for my students. A writer can quickly see how many examples of a particular word (in this case, the single "i") are in the writing and quickly make replacements.

Image 6.2 Using the "Find" Feature to Discover Uses of "i"

With me not having to prompt students, I believe this to be a big engaging factor of the Triple E Framework. The students are essentially shifting their behavior to a point where they are taking ownership of their writing and I don't have to nudge them to look more closely for mistakes they can easily fix themselves. They are creating positive writing habits while using technology.

I also feel that by using something as simple as "find," students are enhancing their learning because they aren't completely worried about getting every single capital letter during the drafting process. They are not getting distracted by minor details they know they can fix using the tool and shortcut given to them when they edit. There is more of a focus on the content, which is more important to me when it comes to their writing. This also leads me to, again, address the spaces where students are writing on a daily basis and how we can also address issues with other elements of capitalization.

Going Further with Capitalization

I can't emphasize enough my point about meeting the students where they are with their use of technology today, especially when it comes to their writing, the spaces they write in, and the audiences that they are writing for. Gretchen Bernabei's *Grammar Keepers* has some excellent mini-lessons that allow me to do just that; throughout her activities surrounding capitalization, she highlights most of the rules that Anderson did with his students. These mini-lessons are great to work through with students.

However, I feel that the spaces that students will typically engage themselves in everyday, such as Facebook or Twitter, are not addressed. So, as with any strategy or lesson that a teacher may discover through reading a professional text, I put my own spin on it where I feel I can meet my students. Please don't feel I am disregarding Bernabei's lessons – they are great. Yet, when it comes to these great lessons provided by other professionals, I want to do what I think will work best with my students and where they are at with their own learning, as well as effectively utilizing the technology they possess and access every day.

So, taking a look at Bernabei's mini-lesson on Proper Nouns and sticking with what my students are typically doing in the first semester, I use the idea of giving students a sentence to read when starting the lesson. Here is the difference for me when I introduce this capitalization rule to my students; I don't use a mentor text from a novel we are reading. Instead, I comb through Facebook posts and Tweets prior to the lesson and try to find posts (my own or from people I know) and use the posts to teach the lesson. It usually isn't hard to find an example (or two, or three!) with the letter "i" standing alone in a social media update. But, if it begins to take too much time, I will use fake Facebook generators such as the ones mentioned in Chapter 4 and create my own sentence for the students to review.

In Image 6.3, I created a sentence using proper nouns so students can see what should be capitalized in a post that they may put on Facebook. In using this type of resource, I would put the fake Facebook post on the projector and after I discuss the rules of punctuation with proper nouns, I ask the students to identify the proper nouns in the example I have given them. Oftentimes, as we are completing this task together, I will pull up the fake Facebook generator I have created and ask for the students' first comment on the post by doing a quick "turn and talk" with a partner, then we come together as a whole class to discuss the things that they notice and if there is anything that should be fixed. Of course, they identify my capitalization and punctuation errors, so I return to the post and edit it, as shown in Image 6.4. This gives the students a sense they are actually writing for Facebook and they become more engaged because we are learning the lesson in their own spaces.

The same can be done with Simitator.com, or other sites where you can create a fake Tweet. Personally, I have found that Facebook seems to be more engaging for the students because more of my students have Facebook accounts, but the approach is still the same whether using the Facebook generator or Twitter.

Image 6.3 Example Post from Facebook to Model Proper Capitalization

Mr. Hyler

I flew to minneapolis minnesota last wednesday to attend an amazing NCTE conference.

Like · Comment · 9 minutes ago ·

👍 24 people like this.

Write a comment ...

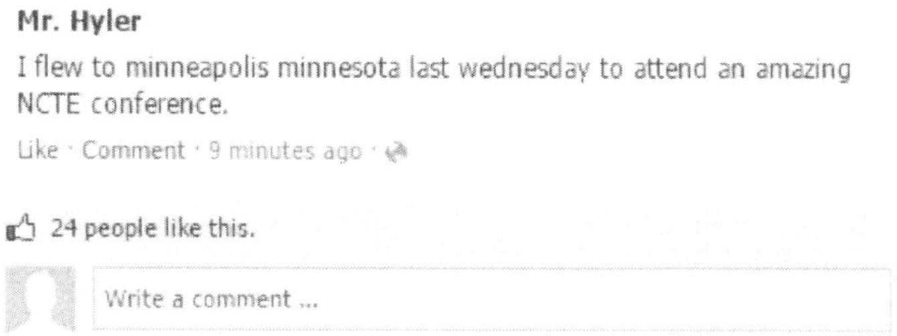

Image 6.4 Corrected Post from Facebook to Model Proper Capitalization

Mr. Hyler

I flew to Minneapolis, Minnesota last Wednesday to attend an amazing NCTE Conference.

Like · Comment · 9 minutes ago ·

👍 24 people like this.

Write a comment ...

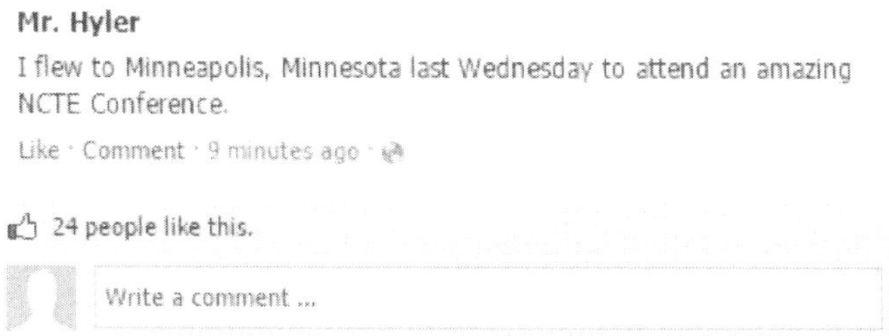

One of the other areas to highlight when doing this type of activity with students is the type of audience they are writing for when posting on social media. Essentially, I want students to think about whether they are writing to friends, family, peers, teachers, future employers, or other unintended audiences. Furthermore, lessons such as these where I am incorporating social media are not forgotten by my students. There are many times students are working on assignments throughout the year. When they are given directions or guidelines, students will make comments such as, "Mr. Hyler, do you mean like how we did it with the social media template?" or "Are we supposed to do it like we did it with the fake texting and Tweeting?" When students are asking questions such as these, I know that the activities that we have done earlier are having an impact and that they are retaining what they have learned.

Though they may seem like minor changes, I believe in meeting my students where they are, and keeping them as engaged as possible – with subject matter that may not only seem elementary to them, but let's face it, boring – is crucial. Adapting a few of these capitalization ideas should help students be more successful in their writing. Capitalization may seem like something minuscule, but when you add the issues students have with punctuation, these two entities together can cause headaches for teachers as they are evaluating student writing.

The Paradox of Punctuation

Punctuation is a huge subtopic of grammar that is obviously part of the CCSS. The two punctuation topics that I see my students struggle with are the comma, and the use of semicolons and colons. The reason I feel my students struggle with these types of punctuation marks is because they don't fully understand the rules, nor do they have enough practice in their writing using these types of punctuation. More importantly, I believe it is because students don't consciously think about using these punctuation marks as options in their writing. That's the paradox: they know about the tools, but simply choose not to use them.

When it comes to punctuation, my students watch flipped videos (Chapter 3) on the rules, and are not only given examples of usage, but I also require them to show me the correct way to use them. Students don't stop there. Quite often, I will have them deliberately use them in their writing at the beginning of class (what I call "writing into the hour") in addition to requiring them to demonstrate the knowledge of the skill in their more thorough writing assignments. Similar to what Anderson describes in

Mechanically Inclined as "an over-do-it backlash" (p. 87), I too experience students over-using the new concepts they get introduced to for a week or so. Honestly, I would rather see this happen instead of students not caring. They are trying, and if they are trying I need to fuel that desire with more engaging lessons other than the flipped lessons. That's where the following lessons come in.

Taking Time to Pause with a Comma

The work I do in my classroom with my students when it comes to implementing technology alongside grammar uses the Triple E Framework. I feel it is vital to think about how a social media tool such as Twitter can not only fit within that framework, but create more competent writers as students advance through middle school to prepare for high school writing.

For the following activity, I feel that Twitter enhances student learning because of the small steps I take; these steps help create an effective scaffold for students to be confident in using commas in their writing. Furthermore, if students are going to use social media outside of school, they are extending their learning through the use of technology, which can't be done with traditional teaching methods.

One of the most common errors students have in their writing is the comma splice. This is when students use a comma and then forget to use a coordinating conjunction. In these cases, students should be using just a period or a semicolon. If students don't understand the semicolon, however, they are not going to use that type of punctuation to correct the error in their writing.

Although the comma can appear to be simple in and of itself, my students struggle with using it. One of the biggest errors that I see in my students' writing is the placement of the comma in their sentence even when there isn't a comma splice. For example: "The moose came near the lake but, he was spooked by the hunter that sat in the tree blind." The rule says that students and writers are supposed to place a comma before the coordinating conjunction. My seventh graders the last two years have had the habit of placing the comma after the conjunction. This is a problem that I want to correct as soon as possible, both because it does not follow the rule and it can cause student writing to lack a sense of flow.

Now, when I start to reinforce the rules for commas, I immediately gravitate towards the social media site Twitter. I do not require my students to sign up for Twitter, but I do send home parent permission forms at the beginning of the year outlining the different digital tools that students will be using during the school year. If parents don't want their child using

Twitter, they simply don't check the box. A link to the parent letter is on the companion wiki for the book. For those students who don't want to use a real Twitter account or may not be able to, they can use Simitator.com other fake Twitter generators mentioned earlier. In the next section I will discuss how I use it for semicolons and colons, too, and how the two lessons can go hand-in-hand.

At the writing of this book, Twitter was still only allowing 140 characters, which is one of the big reasons I like using Twitter for these lessons. Now, if the restriction on the number of characters is lifted, it may cause me to rethink how I teach this lesson. Because students have comma splices in their writing and they need to be fixed, Twitter's brevity can help them with not only minimizing their sentences and requiring them to get to the point, but can also "force" them to use punctuation marks like commas, semicolons, colons, and dashes. In addition, we talk in class about how it is incorrect to use a comma splice.

As an example, here is a sentence I grabbed from a seventh grader's journal: "I walked through the door, I didn't know there would be two different people in costumes ready to scare me." The way the sentence is written now, it includes a comma splice. I give credit to the student for trying to use a comma instead of creating short, choppy sentences. But, it still needs some attention.

So, I pull up my Twitter account so that my students can see it, and I type in the sentence. As I type it in, it is only 107 characters long. I take the time and discuss with my students that there are 33 more characters that could potentially be used in this sentence. Also, we discuss the fact there are two ideas in this comma splice that need to be joined together. Again, I make sure that I give credit to the student for trying to use a comma, but point out that something is missing here.

Then, I ask for revision suggestions. As students are looking at one another and scratching their heads, I ask them to think back to compound sentences and the Schoolhouse Rock video, "Conjunction Junction." When I start to sing the song, the students then realize that there is a conjunction missing and they give me two different ways that the sentence could be written using Twitter. As examples, Images 6.5 and 6.6 are from the fake Twitter website. One of the additional elements that I require my students to do is to display the rule (or rules), briefly, using hashtags.

With the changes the students from Images 6.5 and 6.6 made, each one has created a sentence that displays the correct way to use a comma, and they demonstrate an understanding of what needed to be done by displaying hashtags with the rules. Each student chose to write a different hashtag, but both have grasped the concept and understood what needed to be

Image 6.5 First Sample of Revision on Twitter

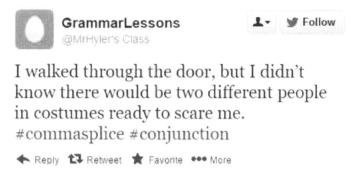

Image 6.6 Second Sample of Revision on Twitter

changed in the sentence. Furthermore, the students stayed with the limited character count. Image 6.5 is 137 characters long and Image 6.6 was 136. Yes, the hashtags do cut down on some of their available space, but I also want students to reflect on the rules that they are learning.

If students want to use the real Twitter site instead of using the simulator, there is something I ask the students to do so I can access examples of their use of commas or other grammar activities that they do in class. I like the students to use a hashtag such as #7fms or #fmsgrammar. This will create the hashtag where students can participate in contributing their own voice and examples which they can access later. Image 6.7 shows two examples where students used the dash. Though these examples are not of comma usage, they both deal with using punctuation to indicate a pause or a break; this connects directly with CCSS language standard 8.2. I use Tweetdeck to see my hashtag columns and the student examples are from that site.

Image 6.7 Sample of the Use of a Dash with Hashtag on Twitter

Though the students are engaged and love the idea of using social media, they do need some incentive to keep practicing these particular grammar skills. Because I am not the "drill and kill" type of teacher (except when it comes to vocabulary . . . sorry!), I require students to give me two or three examples of correct comma usage and put them into the hashtag. It really does depend on where we are with time (both class time and the time of school year) and how well the students are grasping the concept. Regardless of how students' understanding is developed further, it is crucial to point out that students must continue to practice the skill in their writing assignment.

I feel that what I do is simple and to the point, yet teaches students to use social media for more than just saying "hi" to friends or expressing their frustration with school. The next section uses Twitter in a similar matter to help students become more comfortable with using the semicolon.

Is it a Period? Is it a Comma? No, it's a Semicolon!

The semicolon is tricky for middle school students in the sense that they are not confident about using it at all. At the beginning of every year, there are very few students using semicolons in their writing, or, if there are students using them, they don't tend to use them correctly. Sometimes, I feel that the idea is above the heads of my seventh graders, so I tend to save semicolons for eighth grade. Similar to the section above, I use Twitter to help students enhance their learning by helping them gain a more sophisticated understanding of using a semicolon. It isn't simply inserted into a sentence without some type of purpose. Students start to think more clearly about the moves they make as writers when they are using this type of punctuation in their writing.

Semicolons are used to link independent clauses that share similar ideas. It can also be used in a sentence when there too many commas within a sentence. As I begin the lesson with my students, I take six minutes and have my students listen to a Grammar Girl (www.quickanddirtytips.com/education/grammar/semicolons) episode on semicolons (this link is also on our wiki). As mentioned earlier, Grammar Girl is a great resource for students to access when they may need another way for a concept to be explained.

In this particular episode, Grammar Girl (aka, Mignon Fogarty) discusses the idea of using the semicolon to add variety to sentences, a key idea that I want my students to take away. I want my eighth graders to expand their writing repertoire as they prepare for high school. By using the semicolon, students can demonstrate they have a variety of skills in their tool belt to show they are mature writers who are ready to move on to the next level. When we are done listening to the podcast by Grammar Girl, I share a link to a Google Doc with five boxes and I ask my students to work with their group to come up with a definition in their own words on what a semicolon is and how is it used in everyday writing.

When students are done forming definitions, we work together to form our own definition combining the ones that the groups come up with, then the students put that definition along with their other grammar definitions in their grammar folders in Google Docs. As mentioned at the beginning of the book, there will be a few student examples on the companion wiki of a more complete-looking grammar folder that my students have completed. The definition that my students and I came up with this past year was: "Semicolons are used for a break. It can also be used when there are too many commas in a sentence. It connects common ideas."

From this point in our discussion, it is time for the students to start thinking about how they are going to use this new punctuation mark in their own writing. I return to Twitter to have them think about how they are going to use this. So, I give the following example and pose a problem to them.

It really sucks when you want to use your brand new iPhone in class for school, but can't because you did not charge it last night when you get home from the basketball game. #sucks #loser

Josh wants to post a tweet to Twitter but can't because he is at 174 characters, which is well over the 140 characters allowed on Twitter. How can you fix the sentence using a semicolon? Feel free to change the words around, but you do need to make sure there are two independent ideas that are connected.

My students continue to work in their groups and they take the sentence and play around with it. I tell them that they can use any digital tool they want to play around with the sentence. They can use Lino, which we mentioned earlier in the book, or they can simply use a Google Doc to rearrange the sentence and incorporate the semicolon. Many groups use Google Docs because they use the word count feature located in the tools menu. Below are two examples, one from each one of my eighth grade classes last year:

> *My brand new iPhone wasn't charged enough for school; I couldn't use it in class because I needed to save my battery. #sucks* (124 characters)

> *I forgot to charge my new iPhone when I got home from my game last night; I really needed it for class. #drainedbattery (119 characters)*

At this point in the year, what I really appreciate with my students is their willingness to really take a sentence apart and revise it. They aren't just simply taking out an everyday conjunction like "and" and replacing it with the semicolon. I strongly believe that, because they are only given 140 characters to work with, they make more of an effort to actually revise the sentence by adding and deleting words that may or may not be necessary. Twitter's 140-character limit has enhanced their learning by keeping them clear and focused. They are more active in their learning because, instead of just changing one or two words, they are using many steps to revise a sentence. Ultimately, to help students mature as writers, it benefits them if we have multiple, unique ways to help them improve their writing.

Also, you will note that students use hashtags in a different way here, mostly for humor. In this case, because they are simply playing with the idea of the semicolon and I am not formally assessing them, I am willing to let them play around with hashtags as a shorthand way to express emotion or connect to a broader concept instead of indicating the grammar rule or connecting to our hashtag stream.

Extensions and Adaptations

I do care about where and how my students are writing, so I take what they have learned while using the social media tool Twitter and have a conversation with them about how they are going to apply what they have learned to their own writing, no matter what spaces they are going to write in. I quickly create a table (Figure 6.2) in Google Documents for students to access and ask them to fill it in with appropriate responses.

Figure 6.2 Ideas from Our Class Conversation on Commas and Semicolons

Where will the comma and semicolon come in handy for you?	
Commas	Semicolons
I know now that when I am doing my myth I need to make sure I have a coordinating conjunction where I may have a comma splice	*I don't like to type a lot when I text, I could use the semicolon to replace the word and – less typing for me :)*
I never thought about the fact what I was doing was called a comma splice. I could just separate my sentences.	*A semicolon could be used to shorten down the number of characters in Twitter, especially if you didn't have enough.*
I'm thinking Facebook! I don't tend to think about punctuation on Facebook, but I don't want to eat grandma like Mr. Hyler's shirt says. *(Let's eat, Grandma/Let's eat Grandma.)*	*Semicolons can help me when I have too many commas in my sentence and I tend to do that.*

Typically, the table is much bigger because I give each student their own space for them to write their responses. I particularly love the last response under the column for commas. I have a t-shirt that says "Grammar Saves Lives" and it has the two sentences about grandma on it, one of which has a misplaced comma and results in Grandma's untimely demise. I wear it when we are learning about commas, and we have a lively discussion about how we are not cannibals and need to make sure we use our commas appropriately. Students tend to get a kick out of my shirt and how one little punctuation mark can totally change the meaning of the sentence. It is evident that the student who referenced my shirt clearly intends to be more careful about what she puts on Facebook.

Next Steps

As I've noted throughout this book, I want to meet students where they are currently at when it comes to their learning style. I could teach capitalization and punctuation skills in a traditional manner and just mention how one could use these skills through social media, but that doesn't fully engage the students. Besides, we know that moving their learning from worksheets to the real world doesn't happen easily, if at all.

More importantly, I feel that they need to know that I understand the inner workings of the spaces that they write in daily. No, not every student uses Twitter or Facebook, but at some point in their lives, a majority of students are going to be using some kind of short form communication. Perhaps I will have struck a strong enough chord with them in the way that I teach these lessons that they remember not only the rule, but how to apply it to when and where they are writing. Despite their informality, what happens in these spaces is still a linguistic interaction, and students should understand it as such.

Teaching grammar in a digital age is – and will remain – a challenge for us all. Our hope is that the lessons we've described so far have been helpful for you in making that process your own. In our final chapter, we will share four final tips that you can use as you begin to navigate this path on your own.

7

Assessing Grammar in a Digital Age

As is customary in the ending of any book, Troy and I would like to share our final thoughts and reflections here on how grammar is being taught. But, there is a caveat. Personally, I don't claim to be the saving grace or have all the answers; I do know what I am doing is working with my students and I am seeing growth.

Just as many other teacher-writers we've cited in the book – as well as many more that are doing the work with students everyday – we know that there are many ways to help students learn about grammatical concepts. We encourage you to take the time to reflect on your own practices and perhaps find a way to implement something we have discussed into your own classroom.

More importantly, when it comes to teaching grammar in a digital age, we want readers to remember the foundation, the Triple E Framework, when considering what technologies to integrate into the classroom. Throughout each chapter, Troy and I discussed and worked through Liz Kolb's framework to ensure that the tools chosen to integrate with each lesson and activity will positively impact student achievement and their learning outcomes. It's worth reiterating the main questions from the Triple E Framework that have guided our thinking:

◆ *Engage*

  o Does the technology motivate students to start the learning process?

◆ *Enhance*

  o Does the technology create paths for students to demonstrate their understanding of the learning goals in a way that they could not do with traditional tools?

◆ *Extend*

  o Does the technology create a bridge between school learning and everyday life experiences?
  o Does the technology allow students to build skills that they can use in their everyday lives?

Besides making smart decisions about implementing technology, we are hoping that it is evident that the debate about how grammar should be taught may continue for 100 more years, but both of us are convinced that there isn't a single teacher who wants to hear descriptions from his or her students like the ones I mentioned at the beginning of the book, either. Troy and I both know that no one wants to be the teacher of the least favorite class, nor do they want to see their students disenchanted with the subject that they are teaching. In the past, it seems, no matter how grammar has been presented, whether in isolation or within context, our students were just not that interested in grammar lessons. They would do anything to avoid it. Furthermore, when our students aren't interested, we as teachers don't like teaching the topic or we don't look forward to it when it comes up in our curriculum.

There is no doubt grammar often offers us (and our students) that level of displeasure. When thinking about where grammar instruction has been in the past, however, it seems that we are not alone in this battle. Our colleagues have been struggling with the teaching of grammar for decades, and we are likely to continue the debate well into the future. Even with the challenges that face us, we know that the only constant is change; it continues to encompass us in education and we can't afford to sit back and just wonder how we are going to reach our students. Let's take advantage of the continuous evolution of language and move forward in positive, creative ways.

For instance, at the end of this past school year, I found an article in *Teen Ink* titled "Grammar in the Digital Age" where the author Katie Prior argues, "If grammar continues to be enforced strictly, creative possibilities may be destroyed, and the world may never have the opportunity to enjoy a novel that reads with the same depth and complexity as the human voice" (p. 27).

Though Prior raises an interesting argument for not shoving grammar skills down students' throats, she hits on the idea that there should be more creative approaches to the idea of grammar. That is, we cannot freak out every time our students forget to put a capital "I" in their writing. Grammar needs to be taught, there is no arguing that point, but with the ever-changing landscape in which our kids write, we need to think about how we are going to address their needs as learners.

I have shared the idea with colleagues at conferences that my challenge for them is to find two new technologies to integrate into the classroom per year, and to do so with high quality and in different ways. Over the course of five years, a teacher could potentially implement a total of ten new technologies. Also, as a quick side note, don't be afraid to learn these technologies right along with the students – they can teach us the ins and outs of digital tools as well.

So as we continue to learn as teachers, where exactly do we go from here with grammar? Troy and I have discussed these ideas at length, and we will boil it down to four main tips as well as some connections to assessment and student motivation that we share below.

From Texting to Teaching: Four Tips

1. Meet students where they are with the technology and platforms where they typically write on a daily basis.

I have tried to echo this tip throughout the book – probably too much – but if we don't accept the fact that our students are writing in different spaces, and also writing in different ways, we will not be successful in reaching them. Based on both decades of evidence and my own experiences, I know that teaching grammar in isolation simply does not work. Ultimately, as classroom teachers, we will see more pushback from our students if we continue to teach grammar with workshops and drills. Our students know how to code switch – to move in and out of linguistic patterns depending on context – and we have to be willing to guide them when to approaching their use of "digitalk."

2. Stop blaming technology for how our students write and use (or fail to use) grammar today.

Technology is not totally to blame for the grammar problems that seem to be ingrained into our students. For years, teachers have struggled with getting students to understand and apply what they have learned when it comes to grammar skills. Are there new linguistic challenges that our students present to us? Yes, both Troy and I would totally agree (both as teachers and as parents!).

Still, if we think about the invention of the first digital calculator in the 1960s, is that new technology of the time responsible for students being lazy in math? Absolutely not! More students want to use the calculator as a shortcut, but they haven't become worse at math only because of this particular technology. Moreover, most reasonable people don't want to get rid of calculators. As a matter of fact, calculators continue to evolve.

Blaming cellphones, texting, or digital platforms such as Facebook, isn't going to help bridge the gaps that our students have in grammar. Teaching them how to use grammar and to become more sophisticated writers, will.

3. Be creative and innovative with grammar instruction while leaning on other professionals for help.

I love Jeff Anderson and his approaches to grammar. The reason Anderson was good at what he did in his classroom is because he knew it was an area that he needed to strengthen his own knowledge. Like Anderson, I knew I had a lot to learn about grammar, and I also knew I had to be willing to think outside the box and reach more of my students. In turn, I also knew I had to lean on my colleagues and my professional learning network to get ideas and to see if the ideas I had were valid. This book is an evolution of thought based on my on-going professional growth and I will, of course, continue to evolve.

There are two ways that I would encourage anyone interested in teaching writing (and grammar) to grow their own skill set. First, I highly encourage any teacher to access Twitter and join some of the wonderful chats that take place there. The resources that are available are astronomical and teachers want to help each other. I highly recommend #engchat, #mschat, and #teachwriting. Below are the times for these chats.

◆ #engchat – At least one Monday per month (Check the hashtag and the website engchat.org for more information)
◆ #mschat – Typically every Thursday night at 8:00 p.m. Eastern Time
◆ #teachwriting – Every other Tuesday night at 8:00 p.m. Eastern Time (teachwritingchat.org)

Second, as the newly appointed vice-president for NCTE's Assembly for the Teaching of English Grammar (ATEG), I would also encourage anyone to join this group that is solely dedicated to grammar and how grammar is being taught by visiting the website: ateg.weebly.com. The membership is reasonable: $12.00 for one year or $20.00 for two years. They host a yearly conference where there is an open invitation for presenters. Also, they produce the ATEG journal three to four times per year on topics such as:

- Classroom practices in the teaching of grammar
- Traditional vs. linguistic approaches to grammar
- Why and how grammar should or should not be taught
- How we handle language varieties in the classroom
- Teacher education and the teaching of grammar
- Integration of grammar with writing, speech, literature, and all forms of discourse

4. And, yes, have fun with grammar!

Yeah, it sounds simple, but attitude is everything in the middle school world. If you hate it, so will your students. Play with language and make mistakes. Hold a contest, share great examples, and be willing to laugh with your students. Some of them only see the serious side of us because we have mandates and curriculum to get through. (This is the moment where I give a big thumbs down and press my lips together to give a big raspberry!)

Our students need to know we are real people and can have fun with the lessons we are trying to teach them. I love trying new things with my students and showing them that I can at least try to make a topic that seems so boring, really much, much more interesting. Plus, if I fail, they know that I am going to keep trying to reach them where they are and I will honor their feedback to make myself a better teacher.

Overall, Troy and I feel we are at a crucial point in education where teachers have unique opportunities to present material to our students in exciting, yet meaningful ways, through the use of technology. Grammar is just one of numerous subjects where, as Liz Kolb reminds us, we can extend, enhance, and engage our students through the strategic use of technology.

Dealing with Assessments

Given all those tips, we now need to turn to one final topic. We've been able to avoid it for most of the book, but unfortunately assessments are a reality. I speak more specifically of standardized testing. In the state of Michigan, part of my evaluation as a teacher is how well my students do on standardized testing. So, I know I have to get through the curriculum as much as possible. More importantly, I have to make sure my students are applying what they have learned to their assessments. Application can be the tricky part and it often makes teachers nervous because they want students to do well so it reflects their practices. Sadly, we can't always control how our students perform (or want to perform) on standardized assessments, but our classroom assessment practices can, at the very least, help get them prepared.

My hope is that through the work I do with my students through their grammar activities, their on-going collection of strategies in their folders, and their final portfolios, students will not only take risks with new grammar concepts in their writing, but students will understand and retain what they have to know about grammar. Only then can students apply what they have learned to the many arenas where they write, including the assessments they must complete.

More and more, I feel that formative assessment can help our students because it allows us to focus on the problem areas our students are having with their writing, including grammar. When teachers can see what students are understanding and what they are not understanding, teachers and educators can address specific issues and help students make their writing stronger. Furthermore, using assessment ideas such as a digital portfolio can measure the amount of growth students are achieving throughout the year. The following sections outline how I approach the task.

Summative Assessment through Portfolios

Image 7.1 shows an eighth grade portfolio through the first marking period of the year. Using Google Drive, students create a folder and then I get access to all of their writing pieces, including those specifically related to grammar lessons. In the past, I have had students do a reflection piece for their portfolios at the conclusion of each piece of writing as well as at the conclusion of the marking period so they can discuss the growth in their writing and what areas they need to work on as they move forward.

For the 2016–17 school year, I am setting up more of a checklist for essential standards. Essential standards are Common Core State Standards in which students must have attained mastery level in order for them to advance to the next grade. This is a work in progress and I am hoping it can lead to better student achievement with the different types of writing assignments; also, I hope it helps them perform better on standardized assessments. Being a Google Apps for Education school, it is easy to use Google Drive for student writing portfolios. Students can house all of their work on their account and it can easily stay with them when they advance through the grades. Image 7.1 shows a screenshot of a student's drive folder where their writing assignments are placed as a portfolio collection.

Image 7.1 Student Writing Portfolio Shared in a Google Drive Folder

Student Reflections

In addition to the formative and summative assessments, I really feel that it is important for students to reflect on what they have done throughout the year, and at the end of the year.

Students are amazed at what they have learned during the course of a given year. One of the first things my eighth graders do at the start of the school year is complete an introductory piece of writing that highlights who they are and gives me a great sample of their writing at the beginning of their eighth grade year. The only areas I assess my students on are their spelling, capitalization, and punctuation along with their content. It is a simple piece of writing where I am trying to gauge their basic skills.

Upon completing this writing project, I have my students go back and look at a piece of writing from seventh grade and write a reflection piece. Below is an example from a student's writing portfolio. You can clearly see the student feels they have improved as a writer through seventh grade and even at the start of eighth grade. It is amazing to see students' faces when they are reading their writing from the prior year. I bet if they could really express what they are thinking, they may use some very colorful language in their initial thoughts! Thus, reflection sets aside time for students to closely examine their writing and not just look at the grade they earned only to then put it to one side. Then, after the students reflect on their work, they are in the frame of mind to give feedback on the assignments they have completed over the course of the year. Here is one student sample:

<u>8th Grade Intro Writing</u>

1. *What are your initial thoughts after you read this piece of writing?*
    My initial thoughts were: I was only 5′6″?! I could have done something different there. I don't think I was a very good writer. My writing has improved a ton.

2. *How has your writing changed since this piece? Please give two specific examples.*

   My writing has improved significantly, especially with the little things. For example, instead of introducing myself so plainly, I might play around and have a little fun with it now. Another example: When I told people about my award, I drew out the long name of the fair. I might use a shorter name now.

3. *What goals do you have for your writing? List at least 2. Be specific.*

   a. I will try to write about things I like writing about. For example, when we did a student choice writing, I really enjoyed it, because I was not forced to write something I hate.
   b. I will try to keep being creative when I write. When I did the diary, I thought I was very creative.

Students Raise Their Voices: Asking For and Implementing Their Feedback

Now, when it comes to reflecting more specifically on the activities they are doing in my classroom, my students don't have a problem speaking their minds when I ask them to give me feedback about the activities we do, especially surrounding grammar! I'm always working to improve my teaching, but I also know that some students will not be happy with certain elements of class no matter what I do. Still, I want them to know that I am listening, and that I take their questions, concerns, and new ideas seriously.

For instance, below are three questions I ask my students about the "sentence hacking" template (mentioned in Chapter 4), along with two student responses for each question.

1. By completing the grammar template do you have a better understanding of formal vs. informal writing? Explain why you know the difference.

   a. "I do know the difference because it depends on the audience for your writing. It helps me to think about where I am writing."
   b. "Formal writing is the papers I turn into my teachers and I need to not have text talk in that writing. It is okay when I am talking or texting my friends."

2. Do you feel that by completing the template you have a better understanding of adverbs and adjectives and how they are used?

   a. "I know that adjectives and adverbs can completely change the meaning of sentences. It makes me think more about using them in my writing and if my writing makes sense"

b. "The templates help me because it seems more realistic in terms of where I do most of my writing. I am hoping to be able to use less dead words in my writing."

3. How will activities such as the one we did with grammar templates improve your writing?

a. "I never thought about the fact I actually put certain things like adverbs and adjectives in my writing. I might pay attention to them more, especially if Mr. Hyler makes us use them."

b. "I think my writing will be more descriptive and I won't use text talk as much."

I really appreciate my students' honest answers. One additional question that should be asked of students is how to improve an activity. As I mentioned in earlier chapters, students are quick to tell me that they don't use a certain social media platform and it would be better to use, for example, Snapchat instead of Instagram. Overall, students feel that they are getting the skills they need and they are thinking more consciously about the moves they are making as writers when it comes to grammar concepts.

One other option besides Google Drive could be Wikispaces, which is free for educators, and students could create their own page where they house all of their writing assignments. Weebly is also another free site that teachers can utilize for student portfolios. Using Wikispaces or Weebly is useful to house student work because both act more as a traditional website unlike Google Docs. This allows students to share their work more easily with parents, relatives, or other teachers.

By sharing their work more publicly, and with a broader group of people, students are then not only writing for a more authentic audience, but are more conscious about making sure they are making appropriate grammar moves based on what they have learned throughout the year. Furthermore, by teaching my students grammar skills through different social media sites and also teaching them the difference between formal and informal writing spaces, they can apply what they have learned to the different sites and then know how their writing should look depending on whether they are writing a blog post or putting a comment on a discussion board.

Besides using student writing as summative assessments to measure the skills they have learned, do remember that, yes, I give students somewhat traditional quizzes and exams. To make this easier on them and me, I use an online tool where you can create assessments called Socrative (socrative.com). It is a tool where you can create not only quizzes, but also exit tickets or polls to measure student achievement. Formative assessments are just as effective with students as well.

Formative Assessment can also be done with Student Response Systems such as:

◆ Plickers (plickers.com)
◆ Nearpod (nearpod.com)
◆ Click Einstein (clickeinstein.com)
◆ Kahoot (getkahoot.com)

These types of tools can give teachers immediate feedback on whether students are actually understanding the concept or lesson that is being taught. Also, teachers could use the social media tool Celly (cel.ly) with students to turn a traditional exit slip into more of a digital exit slip. It is a safe tool that is educator- and student-friendly. It is free to use and can be used both on cellphones and on computers. I simply create a class within Celly and have students request to join the class (or, as they describe it, a "cell") and then students can submit a response at the end of the hour. It can also be a great tool to communicate with students outside of school. If cellphone policies allow it, the Celly app can be downloaded and used. We outline the use of Celly in more detail in our first book, and have additional links on our wiki (textingtoteaching.wikispaces.com).

Depending on what type of technology is available, you will need to make appropriate decisions on how to assess your students. Again, remember the Triple E Framework and our four tips. For me, I feel fortunate because my school is basically one-to-one and students have access to laptops. In addition, over the past four years, almost 100% of my students have a device or have access to a device where they can complete tasks related to school. So, I have been moving toward more formative assessment as a result. But, even if your time with technology is limited, don't let the technology alone determine if you do more formative or summative assessment in the classroom. Make choices based on how you want to engage, enhance, and extend your students' – as well as your own – learning.

Afterword

Navigating Your Own
Grammatical Journey

As I mentioned in *Create, Compose, Connect!*, it is important to reflect on my practices and think about how I can make them better; I really hope that all teachers are willing to do the same. By no means are my lessons perfect. I want to continue to think about how digital literacies are affecting our students and what I can do to engage them to the fullest. Our hope is that you can find some tidbit to take away from this book. In addition, Troy and I hope that it can help spark a conversation within your own school or personal learning network. There are a few things to keep in mind as you jump in:

Yes, Technology Will Keep Changing. But, Good Teaching is Good Teaching is Good Teaching

Interestingly enough, as we were wrapping up this book, Twitter shut down its six-second looping video service, Vine. And, perhaps by the time the manuscript actually makes its way into print, another one (or two) of the services that we mention in the book will become part of the digital dust heap. That said, we both adhere to the idea that good teaching is, indeed, good teaching; technology, while not neutral in any sense, still should not define the task, for better or for worse. We both remain committed to the idea that educators must think through the learning task first, then think carefully about the technology (or technologies) that could enhance one's teaching.

Still, it is Important to Stay Current . . .

Given the fact that we focus on teaching first, it is still critical that we respond to students' changing technology tastes. For instance, in the social media grammar template (Chapter 4), I have moved from the photo sharing service of Instagram to Snapchat. Now, it seems that my students are back on Instagram, so I may change it again. I don't try to keep up with every single app and game that they use, but I do try to keep my ear to the ground and stay current. As I mentioned earlier, sometimes I just ask them to tell me what they are using and what suggestions they might have for me. I don't always have to adopt the technology into my teaching (or even my template!), but I do want students to know that I am aware of their online worlds.

. . . and, to Find Balance

Here, we mean balance both in terms of grammar instruction and technology integration. First, there has to be more of a delicate balance between the practice of grammar and the implementation of grammar. We know teachers who still teach their students to diagram sentences. That's OK, but only if done with a broader goal of helping students become better writers and scaffolding them in the process. Second, with technology, we see teachers who won't use technology much, if at all; we also see teachers going overboard with many, many new technologies at the expense of focused learning. Balance, as with many things in life, is crucial for us all as we continue to figure out innovative ways for teaching grammar with technology.

As the educational landscape continues to change, I get more and more excited. Call me a nerd, a geek, or techy . . . the new digital tools that emerge every day can give teachers new and exciting ways to engage our students. I am looking forward to continuing work with other educators and discussing the endless possibilities that are still waiting for us as we move away from seeing smartphones as tools for texting and, instead, start using them more and more as tools for teaching.

References

Anderson, J. (2005). *Mechanically Inclined: Building Grammar, Usage, and Style into Writer's Workshop*. Portland, ME: Stenhouse Publishers.

Anderson, J. (2007). *Everyday Editing*. Portland, ME: Stenhouse Publishers.

Anderson, J., & Dean, D. (2014). *Revision Decisions: Talking Through Sentences and Beyond*. Portland, ME: Stenhouse Publishers.

Ash, K. (2012, August 29). Educators Evaluate "Flipped Classrooms." *Education Week*. Retrieved from http://edweek.org/ew/articles/2012/08/29/02el-flipped.h32.html.

Benjamin, A., & Berger, J. (2010). *Teaching Grammar: What Really Works*. New York: Routledge.

Benjamin, A., & Oliva, T. (2007). *Engaging Grammar: Practical Advice for Real Classrooms*. Urbana, IL: National Council of Teachers of English.

Bergmann, J., & Sams, A. (2012). *Flip Your Classroom: Reach Every Student in Every Class Every Day*. Washington: ISTE.

Bernabei, G. (2015). *Grammar Keepers: Lessons That Tackle Students' Most Persistent Problems Once and for All, Grades 4–12*. Thousand Oaks, CA: Corwin Press.

Braddock, R. R., Lloyd-Jones, R., & Schoer, L. A. (1963). *Research in Written Composition*. Whitefish, MT: Literary Licensing, LLC.

Bretzmann, J. (2013). *Flipping 2.0: Practical Strategies for Flipping Your Class*. Bretzmann Group LLC. Retrieved from http://bretzmanngroup.com/?page_id=12.

Classroom Window, & Flipped Learning Network. (2012). Improve Student Learning and Teacher Satisfaction in One Flip of the Classroom. Retrieved from http://flippedlearning.org/cms/lib07/VA01923112/Centricity/Domain/41/classroomwindowinfographic7-12.pdf.

Common Core State Standards Initiative. (2010). Common Core State Standards Initiative | The Standards | English Language Arts Standards. Retrieved from http://corestandards.org/the-standards/english-language-arts-standards.

Council of Writing Program Administrators, National Council of Teachers of English, & National Writing Project. (2011, January). Framework for Success in Postsecondary Writing. Retrieved from http://wpacouncil.org/framework.

Drouin, M., & Davis, C. (2009). "R u txting? Is the Use of Text Speak Hurting Your Literacy?" *Journal of Literacy Research*, 41(1), 46–67. Retrieved from http://doi.org/10.1080/10862960802695131.

Education Northwest. (2014, April 16). Trait Definitions [Text]. Retrieved from http://educationnorthwest.org/traits/trait-definitions.

Flipped Learning Network (FLN). (2014) The Four Pillars of F-L-I-P™. Retrieved from http://flippedlearning.org/wp-content/uploads/2016/07/FLIP_handout_FNL_Web.pdf.

Freedman, T. (2011, October 20). 8 Observations on Flipping the Classroom. Retrieved from http://ictineducation.org/home-page/2011/10/20/8-observations-on-flipping-the-classroom.html.

Graham, S., & Perin, D. (2007). *Writing Next: Effective Strategies to Improve Writing of Adolescents in Middle and High Schools*. New York: Carnegie Corporation of New York, p. 77. Retrieved from http://all4ed.org/files/WritingNext.pdf.

Haussamen, B. (2003). *Grammar Alive!: A guide for Teachers*. Urbana, IL: National Council of Teachers of English.

Hicks, T. (2009). *The Digital Writing Workshop* (1st ed.). Portsmouth, NH: Heinemann.

Hillocks, G. (1986). *Research on Written Composition: New Directions for Teaching*. Urbana, IL: National Council of Teachers of English.

Hinton, S. E. (1967). *The Outsiders*. New York: Viking Press.

Hoffman, M. J. (2008). "Echoes of Acrimony: Decades of Grammar Disputes." *Academic Exchange Quarterly*, 12, 126–130.

Hyler, J., & Hicks, T. (2014). *Create, Compose, Connect! Reading, Writing, and Learning with Digital Tools*. New York: Routledge.

Kenkel, J., & Yates, R. (2003). "A Developmental Perspective on the Relationship between Grammar and Text." *Journal of Basic Writing*, 22(1), 35–49.

Key Shifts in English Language Arts | Common Core State Standards Initiative. (n.d.). Retrieved from http://corestandards.org/other-resources/key-shifts-in-english-language-arts.

Killgallon, D. (1997). *Sentence Composing for Middle School: A Worktext on Sentence Variety and Maturity*. Portsmouth, NH: Boynton/Cook.

Killgallon, D. (1998). *Sentence Composing for High School: A Worktext on Sentence Variety and Maturity*. Portsmouth, NH: Boynton/Cook.

Killgallon, D., & Killgallon, J. (2000). *Sentence Composing for Elementary School: A Worktext to Build Better Sentences*. Toronto, ON: Pearson Education Canada.

Killgallon, D., & Killgallon, J. (2012). *Paragraphs for High School: A Sentence-Composing Approach*. Portsmouth, NH: Heinemann.

Killgallon, D., & Killgallon, J. (2013). *Paragraphs for Middle School: A Sentence-composing Approach : a Student Worktext*. Portsmouth, NH: Heinemann.

Killgallon, D., & Killgallon, J. (2014). *Paragraphs for Elementary School: A Sentence-Composing Approach*. Portsmouth, NH: Heinemann.

Kirch, C. (2014). WSQing. Retrieved from https://flippingwithkirch.blogspot.com/p/wsqing.html.

Kolb, L. (2011). Triple E Framework. Retrieved from http://tripleeframework.com.

Lenhart, A. (2015, April 9). Teens, Social Media & Technology Overview 2015. Retrieved from http://pewinternet.org/2015/04/09/teens-social-media-technology-2015.

Lowry, L. (1999). *The Giver*. New York: Bantam Books for Young Readers.

Melamed, S. (2016, March 16). "Kids Who Survived Adult Jail Send a Lifeline to Those Still Inside." Philly.com. *The Inquirer Daily News*. Retrieved from http://philly.com/philly/living/20160316_Kids_who_survived_adult_jail_send_a_lifeline_to_those_still_inside.html.

National Commission on Excellence in Education. (1983, April). A Nation at Risk: The Imperative for Educational Reform. Retrieved from http://datacenter.spps.org/uploads/SOTW_A_Nation_at_Risk_1983.pdf.

National Council of Teachers of English. (1985). Resolution on Grammar Exercises to Teach Speaking and Writing. Retrieved from http://ncte.org/positions/statements/grammarexercises.

NCTE's Assembly for the Teaching of English Grammar. (2002). Guideline on Some Questions and Answers about Grammar. Retrieved from http://www.ncte.org/positions/statements/qandaaboutgrammar.

Newsela | Sports World Loses Boxing Great Muhammad Ali at Age 74. (2016, June 6). Retrieved from https://newsela.com/articles/obit-muhammad-ali/id/18394.

Noden, H. R. (1999). *Image Grammar: Using Grammatical Structures to Teach Writing.* Portsmouth, NH : Heinemann.

Noden, H. R. (2011). *Image Grammar: Teaching Grammar as Part of the Writing Process* (2nd ed.). Portsmouth, NH : Heinemann.

O'Hare, F. (1973). *Sentence Combining: Improving Student Writing Without Formal Grammar Instruction* (ED073483, Vol. NCTE Research Report No. 15). NCTE.

Prior, Katie. "Grammar in the Digital Age." *Teen Ink* Mar. 2016: 27. Print.

Ruday, S. (2014). *The Common Core Grammar Toolkit: Using Mentor Texts to Teach the Language Standards in Grades 6–8.* New York: Routledge.

Shannon, P. (2013). *Closer Readings of the Common Core: Asking Big Questions About the English/Language Arts Standards* (1st ed.). Portsmouth, NH: Heinemann.

Shaughnessy, M. P. (1977). *Errors and Expectations: A Guide for the Teacher of Basic Writing.* New York: Oxford University Press.

Smith, M. W., & Wilhelm, J. (2007). *Getting It Right: Fresh Approaches to Teaching Grammar, Usage, and Correctness.* New York: Scholastic Teaching Resources.

Stanovich, K. E. (1986). "Matthew Effects in Reading: Some Consequences of Individual Differences in the Acquisition of Literacy." *Reading Research Quarterly*, *21*(4), 360–407.

Swayne, M., & Messer, A. E. (2012, July 25). No LOL Matter: Tween Texting May Lead to Poor Grammar Skills. Retrieved from http://news.psu.edu/story/147778/2012/07/25/no-lol-matter-tween-texting-may-lead-poor-grammar-skills.

Taylor, M. D. (1976). *Roll of Thunder, Hear My Cry.* New York: Dial Press.

The Telegraph. (2012, July 27). Texting is Fostering Bad Grammar and Spelling, Researchers Claim. Retrieved from http://telegraph.co.uk/education/educationnews/9432222/Texting-is-fostering-bad-grammar-and-spelling-researchers-claim.html.

Texas Reading Initiative. (2002). *Promoting Vocabulary Development: Components of Effective Vocabulary Instruction.* Texas Education Agency. Retrieved from https://education.ucf.edu/mirc/Research/TRA%20-%20Promoting_Vocabulary_Development.pdf.

Thurlow, C. (2006). From Statistical Panic to Moral Panic: The Metadiscursive Construction and Popular Exaggeration of New Media Language in the Print Media. *Journal of Computer-Mediated Communication*, *11*(3), 667–701. Retrieved from http://doi.org/10.1111/j.1083-6101.2006.00031.x.

Topping, D. (2006). *Getting Grammar: 150 New Ways to Teach an Old Subject.* Portsmouth, NH: Heinemann.

Turner, K. H. (2009). "Flipping the Switch: Code-Switching from Text Speak to Standard English." *English Journal*, *98*(5), 60–65.

Turner, K. H. (2012). "Digitalk as Community." *English Journal*, *101*(4), 37–42.

Turner, K. H., Abrams, S. S., Katíc, E., & Donovan, M. J. (2014). "Demystifying Digitalk The What and Why of the Language Teens Use in Digital Writing." *Journal of Literacy Research*, *46*(2), 157–193. Retrieved from http://doi.org/10.1177/1086296X14534061

Weaver, C. (1979). *Grammar for Teachers: Perspectives and Definitions*. Urbana, IL: National Council of Teachers of English.

Weaver, C. (1996). *Teaching Grammar in Context*. Portsmouth, NH: Boynton/Cook Publishers.

Weaver, C., & Bush, J. (2008). *Grammar to Enrich & Enhance Writing*. Portsmouth, NH: Heinemann.

Wheeler, R. S., & Swords, R. (2004). "Codeswitching: Tools of Language and Culture Transform the Dialectally Diverse Classroom." *Language Arts, 81*(6), 470.

Wilde, S. (2012). *Funner Grammar: Fresh Ways to Teach Usage, Language, and Writing Conventions, Grades 3–8*. Portsmouth, NH: Heinemann.

Wilhelm, J. D., Smith, M., & Fredricksen, J. E. (2012). *Get it Done! Writing and Analyzing Informational Texts to Make Things Happen*. Portsmouth, NH: Heinemann.